Statistics Lecture Notes

Dr. Alex Waigandt
University of Missouri
Health and Exercise Science

KENDALL/HUNT PUBLISHING COMPANY
4050 Westmark Drive   Dubuque, Iowa 52002

This has been printed directly from camera-ready copy.

Copyright © 1995 by Kendall/Hunt Publishing Company

ISBN 0-7872-0450-1

All rights reserved. No part of this publication may be reproduced, stored in a retrieval system, or transmitted, in any form or by any means, electronic, mechanical, photocopying, recording, or otherwise, without the prior written permission of the copyright owner.

Printed in the United States of America
10 9 8 7 6 5 4 3 2 1

Hints for STATWORKS on the Macintosh

1. If you are not familiar with the Mac or how to use a mouse you may want to spend an hour or so practicing on "Mac down Mainstreet." It's available at the desk in Hill 201.

2. If you are using a computer in A&S or in Hill 201 with a hard drive, you don't need a STATWORKS disk or a start-up disk. If you are using a computer without a hard drive, you will need both. In any case, you do not need a data disk--all the data you need to save will fit on your STATWORKS disk. Some people buy a data disk and make it into a start-up disk. You may do this if you wish. The lab consultants in Hill 201 can show you how. You need to be aware that if you plan to use a campus computer somewhere other than Hill 201, you may have to use the start-up disk available at that site.

3. Read the documentation on the STATWORKS program. It will give you information about entering and analyzing data.

4. If you have trouble getting started, the lab consultants will help you.

5. In the event you run into any problems, feel free to contact me or the GTA during office hours.

Dr. Waigandt

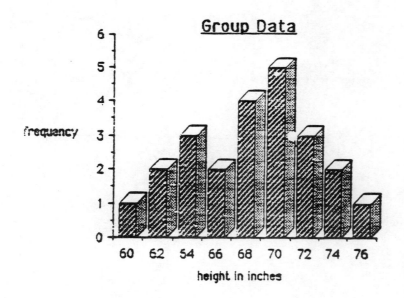

Help Guide for Statistics Program Utilizing the Macintosh Computer

I. QUICK MENU GUIDE

Data

Sort
The Sort command sorts the rows of data in order according to the column you specify.

Recode...
You may use Recode to group a range of numbers into a single numerical code.

Transform...
The Transform command performs a mathematical transformation on a column of data.

2-Column Transform...
Two-Column Transform allows you to add, subtract, multiply or divide a variable by a constant or another variable.

Random Numbers
The Random Numbers command will cause pseudo-random numbers to be created and placed in the next empty column.

Format
Format allows you to choose output notation (scientific or fixed decimal notation, and the number of digits). It also allows you to change the size of characters in the data window.

Stats

Descriptive
Descriptive statistics provide a numerical summary of the distribution of the data.

Cross-Tabulation
Cross-Tabulation describes the overall frequency of occurrence in a class described by two variables containing the classifications.

t-Test
T-tests are used to compare two sample means. Single variable, paired variables and two independent variables may be used in t-tests.

Spearman Correlation
Spearman's rho is used to determine whether two sets of data are related. This test is a nonparametric test and is based on the ranks of the data.

Regression

Simple
Simple regression measures the relationship between one independent variable and one dependent variable.

Anova

1-way Analysis
One-way Analysis of Variance compares means of several samples in a single analysis.

Plot

Scatter
A Scatter plot shows one variable plotted against another in two dimensional space.

Line
Line plots are identical to scatter plots, except that a line is drawn through the data points.

Histogram
A histogram provides a graphical representation of the frequency distribution of a variable.

II. INTRODUCTION TO STATWORKS^{tm}

Statistical computations were among the first uses of the computer. Until StatWorks, however, personal computer users had to wend their way through a sea of often cryptic documentation, or learn new "higher level" languages.

StatWorks is designed for statisticians, physical scientists, biological scientists, social scientists, psychologists, students, and others who conduct statistical analyses in their work.

Compared with Mainframe Packages
The range of statistical procedures found in StatWorks is not as wide as in a mainframe environment, but the procedures most users will need are in StatWorks. One obvious advantage of StatWorks is its highly interactive nature.

Compared with other Micro Packages
Compared with other microcomputer statistical packages, StatWorks is fast, accurate, and very easy to use.

Many microcomputer packages (as well as mainframe packages) require users to go through several stages to complete a statistical analysis. In StatWorks, everything is as

automatic as possible. For instance, when some packages perform an analysis of variance the user must create dummy variables to represent the categories. StatWorks automatically generates the dummy variables for you.

Importance of Graphics
Graphic representation of your data can be extremely important. Humans have an uncanny ability to understand things presented in visual form. StatWorks makes a wide variety of graphics output readily available to you.

Accuracy
Of what value is a statistical result if it is incorrect? Many microcomputer packages, and even a few mainframe packages, suffer from inaccuracies due to roundoff problems (they only calculate results to 7-14 significant digits). StatWorks performs all calculations with 19 significant digits (that is 80 bits of precision) according to the numeric standards established by the IEEE Computer Society and used in Apple Computer's Standard Apple Numeric Environment (SANE).

Caution
Some Knowledge of statistics is necessary in order to understand the wide range of statistical output created by StatWorks. The burden of selecting the proper analysis for a specific set of data is, and always has been, the responsibility of the user.

III. THE DATA WINDOW

Introduction
You enter data into StatWorks through the data window. This window is somewhat like a piece of paper that has been ruled with columns. Entering and editing data, whether numbers of characters, in StatWorks is very consistent with the ease of use typical of the Macintosh. The data window is a cross between a spreadsheet and a word processor.

Basic Structure of the Data Window
The basic structure behind the StatWorks data window is the column format.

Data collected for a variable is entered down a column. The data window may contain up to 35 columns (variables). Each variable may be given a name that is meaningful to you and entered in the box provided at the head of each column. You will also note that across the top of the data window, each column has a number. This is to help you keep track of where you are in a large set of data with lots of columns. Running along the left edge are row numbers. They will also help you keep track of your location in a large data set.

Entering a Column of Data
When no data is present in the window, only one column is labeled and marked. To enter data, click on the column. A flashing vertical line called an insertion bar will appear at the top of the empty column. This insertion bar is your indication of where entry of editing will take place. Go ahead and type your first data value. After you are finished typing the value, press the RETURN key. The insertion bar will now appear on the next line in the column.

Entering Missing Values
Suppose you have a data set that has a missing value for the case that you are entering. Simply push RETURN (or TAB, whichever is appropriate) to enter no value for that case.

Editing Data
The simplest way to correct an erroneous data point is to click just after the data point and then backspace over the data.

IV. THE FILE MENU

New
The New command opens a new, untitled data window.

Open
The Open command opens an existing data set on the disk.

Close
The Close command closes the currently active window. If you close a data window in which changes have been made to the data, a dialog box will ask you if you wish to save the changes.

Save
The Save command stores the data in the active data window on disk for later recall.

Save As...
The Save As command is used to save a data set on disk under a new name or on a different disk.

Print
The Print command produces a printed copy of the currently active window using the settings specified in Page Setup and Print Setup. Choosing this command will print either graphics or text on the printer.

Quit
The Quit command exits StatWorks and returns to the Finder. If any changes were made to the data, you will be asked if you wish to save the changes before returning to the Finder.

V. STATISTICS

Descriptive
Descriptive statistics provide a numerical summary of the distribution of the data. These statistics can be divided into two types: statistics of location and statistics of dispersion. The statistics of location describe the central tendency of the sample distribution. The statistics of dispersion measure the spread of the sample distribution.

Descriptive statistics may be run on any numerical data. However, the statistics are meaningful only if the data is continuous.

Cross-Tabs
Cross-Tabulation computes the frequency of occurrence of all possible combinations of the levels between two categorical variables. StatWorks produces a two-dimentional table to describe the overall frequencies.

Only categorical data are used with this technique.

A number of useful statistical values are displayed, including Chi-square (x^2) and its significance level. The x^2 value measures the statistical independence of the rows and columns of the table.

t-Test
To compare sample means you may use Student's t-Test. There are three types of comparisons that you may wish to do. First, you may want to compare the mean of a collected sample with a hypothesized value. This is referred to as a one sample t-test. A second type of comparison may be made on two paired samples, such as a measurement made before and after a change. Lastly, you may wish to compare the means of two independently collected (unpaired) samples.

Spearman Correlation
Spearman's rho is used to assess the correlation between two variables. This test is a nonparametric test, which uses the ranks of the data instead of their actual values.

Regression

Simple
Simple regression involves the most basic regression model:

$Y_i = aX_i + b + error$

You may at some time need or encounter other regression models which look a little different from the expression above, yet describe the relation between a single dependent and a single independent variable.

Anova

Analysis of variance techniques compare the means of several variables in a single analysis.

ANOVA is used with one or more groups of categorical data and one dependent variable.

1-way Analysis

In one-way ANOVA, groups of samples are classified by only a single factor. Therefore, to complete a one-way ANOVA, you need to specify a variable which contains the class into which the measurement falls and the associated dependent value that was observed.

After selecting 1-way Analysis from the ANOVA menu, you must select the name of the dependent variable. Then you select the name of your independent variable, the data column that contains the classifications, in the box on the right marked "Factor." Since this is a one-way ANOVA, it is appropriate to select only one set of classifications and therefore only one variable name.

An ANOVA table will appear. A standard format for displaying the ANOVA table has been chosen to be consistent with the greatest number of textbooks. Most standard statistics textbooks contain thorough discussions of how to interpret an ANOVA table.

R370 Homework

Microcomputing is one of the most exciting developments within the last 50 years. The disk I have provided for you is designed for the Macintosh microcomputer. The MAC is one of the most versatile of the the new generation microcomputers and also one of the most user friendly (computer talk meaning even you and I can use it) machines available.

On the disk I have provided, you will find the program is called "STATWORKS". This program will allow you to run the data analyses we will do in the classroom.

Your first assignment will involve the use of the software on your disk. Follow the directions in order below. After you have finished, feel free to experiment with the program.

1. Turn on the computer.

2. Insert your disk. (The computer should give you a smiling face, indicating that your disk has been accepted.) In a few seconds your programs will appear on the screen.

3. To access the program. Double click "STATWORKS".

4. Some columns will appear. You will note that the flashing cursor is situated on the top of the first column. Now type the following imaginary data (let's make believe that they represent the heights of 48 students): (Make sure to hit the return key after each entry.) 69, 69, 68, 68, 75, 74, 74, 73, 73, 72, 71, 71, 70, 70, 70, 70, 70, 70, 70, 70, 69, 69, 69, 72, 72, 71, 71, 69, 69, 68, 68, 72, 71, 71, 71, 68, 68, 67, 67, 67, 67, 66, 66, 65, 73, 73, 72, 72.

5. To name the column, bring the mouse to the column heading and click once. Hit the delete button, then type in an appropriate name. In this case the word "height" should do.

6. So that you can get a good visual understanding of your data, let's place them into descending order. This is done by bringing the cursor to "Data", drag to "Sort". Bubble-in "descending order", click "Height" and click, "OK".

7. To save. After you have typed something, bring the mouse up to the word "File" and hold down the button on the mouse. You will note words appear such as "Save", "Print", etc. Drag the mouse down to "Save", release the button and when the box appears, print the words "data 1" (indicating that this is your first data assignment). Bring the mouse to "Save" and click once. In a couple of seconds, you will note that where it used to say "Untitled" it now says "data 1". You have just successfully saved your first document.

8. To plot. Bring the mouse to "Plot", drag down to "Histogram" and release. Put the mouse on "Column 1" and click once. Now put the mouse on "Plot" and click once. Again, if all goes well,

you have just plotted your first histogram.

9. To print your histogram. Bring the mouse to the "File" menu. Drag to print and release. Put the mouse on "OK". The printer should print your histogram.

10. To Shut down. After printing, put the mouse on "File", drag to "Quit" and release. When the main menu appears, put the mouse on "Special" and drag down to "Shutdown".

11. You are now free to experiment with your program.

R370 Homework

During the course of the semester, we will have the opportunity to perform a number of analyses for evaluation. So that you will get a sense of how to enter data and perform functions, we will go through some of them now. During the semester, you will develop an understanding of their meaning (you are not expected to understand them now).

1. Enter the following height and weight data and identify the columns appropriately.

Student number	Height (column 1)	Weight (column 2)
1	75	210
2	74	205
3	74	190
4	73	195
5	73	190
6	73	185
7	73	185
8	72	180
9	72	180
10	72	175
11	72	185
12	72	175
13	72	175
14	71	175
15	71	175
16	71	170
17	71	180
18	71	175
19	71	170
20	71	165
21	70	165
22	70	165
23	70	160
24	70	160
25	70	155
26	70	155
27	70	150
28	70	150
29	69	150
30	69	150
31	69	145

32	69	145
33	69	145
34	69	140
35	69	140
36	68	135
37	68	135
38	68	135
39	68	135
40	68	130
41	68	130
42	67	135
43	67	130
44	67	125
45	67	120
46	66	115
47	66	110
48	65	105

2. Under "Data", "Transform" both columns to z-scores, **print** them and then delete the z-score columns.

3. Under "Data", "Sort" column 2 into descending order and **print**.

4. Under "Data", using the "2-column transformation" program, add columns 1 and 2, **print**, then delete the sum column.

5. Under "Stats" perform "Descriptive" statistics on column 1, **print**.

6. Under "Stats" perform "Descriptive" statistics on column 2, **print**.

7. Under "Regression" perform a "simple regression" using "Height" as the dependent variable and "Weight" as the independent variable. **Print** the "untitled data" figure and the "Anova" table.

8. Under "Plot" conduct a "line" graph using "Height" as the vertical axis and "Weight" as the horizontal axis. **Print**.

9. You are now free to experiment with your programs.

in class
X

R 370 Questionnaire

1. Gender _____

2. Age (in years) _____

3. Eye Color _____

4. Hair Color _____

5. Year in School _____

6. GPA _____

7. Height (in inches) _____

8. Weight (in pounds) _____

9. Major _____

10. How intimidated are you by statistics? (please circle)

    1 2 3 4 5 6 7 8 9 10
  not   extremely
  intimidated   intimidated
  at all

11. How many hours are you enrolled in this semester? _____

Why statistics?

Comments about Research.

What you should get out of this course?
1.

2.

3.

Definition of Terms:

1. **Variable:** A characteristic that takes on different values.

2. **Data** are measurements collected.

   1. Nominal data= name/categorical

   2. Ordinal= ordering/ranking (lined up by height - 1st, 2nd, 3rd, etc. in algebra it is expressed as A less than B (A<B) or A greater than B (A>B)

   3. Interval= number/space between each number is equal (scores)

   4. Ratio= common unit of measurement as with interval and a true zero point so that statements of equality can be made.

3. **Datum:** Is singular of data.

4. **Parameter:** is a description of a population denoted by Greek letters.

5. **Statistic:** Is a number which summarizes data collected on any part of a population (a sample).

   2 types of statistics:

   1. Descriptive
   2. Inferential

   2 types of inferential statistics:

   1. Parametric
   2. Non-parametric

6. **Population** is a complete set of measurements of any characteristic.

7. **Sample** is a subset of the population.

Name:_____

Mini-design assignment

For each of the following questions, identify the main variables and indicate the characteristics of each.

1. Do persons from Arizona, California and Nevada have the same knowledge about current events?

2. Is number of pounds overweight related to systolic blood pressure?

3. Do persons in this class know more about statistics than the average college senior?

4. Is sex related to attitudes towards environmental responsibility?

5. Are children in single-parent families more likely to be delinquents than those that are in dual-parent families?

6. Does anti-hypertension medication reduce a patient's potassium concentration in blood?

7. Do recreation majors have differing levels of approval for wilderness preservation than non-recreation majors?

8. Do persons with high anxiety have high scores on competitiveness?

9. Is brand of analgesic purchased related to knowledge about drugs?

10. Do persons with high anxiety have better reasoning ability than those with low anxiety?

Graphs and Frequency distributions

Graphs are ways to organize data in some systematic fashion.

1. **Raw Data** not very meaningful

2. **Frequency distribution of heights.** more meaningful

3. **Group frequency distribution by class interval.** To get interval width, take the range and divide by the desired # of intervals. If I want 8 intervals, I will ÷ 18 (range) by 8 & get 2.25. We round to 2 units of measurement.

4. **Cumulative frequency and cumulative percentage distributions.** see examples on yellow pad

5. **Bar graphs and histograms** help visually clarify data

6. **Frequency curve** — joining the midpoints of bars in graphs used because you can fit a curve to it

7. **Forms of frequency curves.**

   (Bell) Normal → (egalitarian distribution)

   Leptokurtic → middle is very high (homogenous group)

   (Bell) Mesokurtic →

   Platykurtic → Broad range within the distribution. The more heterogenous — the wider the distribution

   Bi-modal → two groups graphed as one (not very desirable)

   Positively skewed → median preceeds mean
   (median, mean)

   Negatively skewed → mean preceeds median
   (x̄ mean, median)

17

Homework

1. Create a bar graph depicting the frequencies of class membership in R370 for members in the following academic majors:

2. For the following frequency distribution of ages of 87 members, draw a histogram.

Class interval	f
43-48	7
38-42	15
33-37	25
28-32	18
23-27	13
17-22	9

3. For the frequency distribution of scores described in question #2, draw a frequency curve.

4. Describe the types of distributions you would expect if you were to graph each of the following:

   a. annual incomes of American families

   b. the heights of American males

   c. the heights of American females

   d. the heights of American males and females combined in one graph

PERCENTILE RANKS (measuring group position)

✳ Percentile ranks indicate the relative position of an individual in a group. It is the number that represents the percentage of cases in a comparison group which achieve scores at or lower than the one cited.

PERCENTILE RANK AT A GIVEN SCORE

$$\text{Percentile rank} = \frac{\text{cum} f_{ll} + \left(\frac{X - X_{ll}}{i}\right)(f_i)}{N} \times 100$$

where: $\text{cum } f_{ll}$ = cumulative frequency at the lower real limit of the interval containing X
X = given score
X_{ll} = score at lower real limit of interval containing X
i = width of the interval
f_i = number of cases within the interval containing X

SCORE AT A GIVEN PERCENTILE RANK

$$\text{Score} = X_{ll} + \frac{i(\text{cum } f - \text{cum } f_{ll})}{f_i}$$

where:
$\text{cum } f$ = cumulative frequency of the score = cum f = (percentile rank x N)/100
X_{ll} = score at the lower real limit of the intval containing cum f
i = width of the interval
$\text{cum } f_{ll}$ = cumulative frequency at the lower real limit of the interval containing cum f
f_i = number of cases within the interval containing cum f

PERCENTILE RANK HOMEWORK

1. Calculate the percentile rank for your own height.

2. If your percentile rank was 50, what would your height be in inches?

MEASURES OF CENTRAL TENDENCY

(data tend to gravitate to a central value.)

Measure of central tendency

✶ is the index of central location employed in the description of frequency distributions.

THE ARITHMETIC MEAN *(most valuable)*

(Why is the mean the most valuable — it is the arithmetic average of all scores — allows us to describe other measures around it. Further calculations can be made on other data once this is known.)

$$\mu \text{ or } M = \frac{X_1 + X_2 + X_3 \ldots X_n}{N} = \frac{\Sigma X}{N}$$

where: μ or M = the mean is referred to as X bar
  N = number of scores
  Σ = (sigma) the mathematical verb directing us to sum all the measures
  X_{1-n} = individual scores

THE WEIGHTED MEAN

The sum of the mean of each group multiplied by its respective weight (the N in each group), divided by the sum of the weights (total N).

The weighted mean can be expressed as the sum of the mean of each group multiplied by its respective weight divided by the sum of the weights.

$$M_w = \frac{\Sigma(w \times M)}{\Sigma w}$$ *(see notes)*

THE MEDIAN

The score or potential score in a distribution of scores, above and below which one-half of the frequencies fall.

$$MDN = X_{ll} + (i)\frac{N/2 - \text{cum } f_{ll}}{f_i}$$

where: X_{ll} = score at the real lower limit of the interval containing X
i = width of class interval
$cumf_{ll}$ = cum frequency at th lower real limit of the class containing X
f_i = number of cases within the class containing X

MODE

Is the score which occurs with the greatest frequency.

COMPARISON OF THE MEDIAN AND MEAN

report mean on normal distribution, *report median if there is a skew*

MEAN, MEDIAN AND SKEWEDNESS

outstanding characteristic of median — median is insensitive to extreme scores.

CENTRAL TENDENCY HOMEWORK

1. Using your calculator, calculate the mean and median for our class GPA.

2. Using the STATWORKS program, calculate the mean for our class weights. *(show printout for credit)*

3. Say I have been teaching English for five years. My final examination scores for each year and the number of students I have had in each year are as folows:

YEAR	SCORE	# OF STUDENTS
1991	56	23
1992	52	32
1993	58	28
1994	59	29
1995	61	25

Calculate the weighted mean for all of the years I have taught English.

(interval of 10)

9. Calculate the percentile rank for your own weight.

$$PR = \frac{cumf_{ll} + \left(\frac{X - X_{ll}}{i}\right)(f_i)}{N} \times 100$$

$$\frac{125 - 119.5}{10} \, 100$$

10. If your percentile rank was 25, what would your weight be?

$$\frac{25\cancel{\,.98} = 3.42}{75}$$

Homework:

1. What is the term for a characteristic of a population that is measurable? ~~data~~ parameter

2. A number resulting from the manipulation of raw data according to acceptable procedures is a _statistic_.

3. Is the symbol N, representing the number of observations, a verb, ~~adjective~~, adverb, or noun? Noun — learn p. 26 from big book

4. Round the number 15.00500 to the second decimal place. 15.01

5. Using the program, calculate the mean for our class weights. (show printout for credit) 153 (attached to homework)

6. My percentile rank is 87. Tell me what that means. 87% of the people scored at or below you.

7. If the mean and the median is equal, what does that tell you about the distribution? normal curve

8. True or false. $\Sigma X = M(N)$ true

9. Calculate the percentile rank for your own weight.

10. If your percentile rank was 25, what would your weight be?

11. Using your calculator, calculate the mean and median for our class GPA. 3.42   3.425

12. Say I have been teaching for four years. My final examination scores for each year and the number of students I have had in each year are as folows:

YEAR	SCORE	# OF STUDENTS
1988	52	32
1989	58	28
1990	59	29
1991	61	25

$\bar{X}$ 52   58   59   61
N 32   28   29   25

Calculate the weighted mean for all of the years I have taught. 57.23

Measures of Variability

Dispersion = The spread of variability of scores about the measure of central tendency.

Measures of Variability:

1. Range
2. Semi-interquartile range or deviation
3. Mean deviation
4. Variance
5. Standard Deviation

RANGE

The measure of disperion or the scale difference between the largest and the smallest score.

High Score - low score

SEMI INTERQUARTILE RANGE (DEVIATION)

A measure of variability obtained by subtracting the score at the 25th percentile from the score at the 75th percentile and dividing by 2.

$Q_3 - Q_1 / 2$ = semi-interquartile range

MEAN DEVIATION

Sum of the deviations of each score from the mean without regard to sign, divided by the number of scores.

$$M.D. = \frac{\sum (IX - MI)}{N}$$

VARIANCE

The variance is defined verbally as the sum of the squared deviations from the mean divided by N. Symbolically it is represented as

$$S^2 = \frac{\sum(X-M)^2}{N}$$

The variance can also be expressed as $S^2 = SS/N$

STANDARD DEVIATION

An extremely useful measure of dispersion defined as the square root of the sum of the squared deviations from the mean, divided by N.

$$SD = \sqrt{SS/N}$$

The definitional formula is:

$$SD = \sqrt{\frac{\sum(X-M)^2}{N}}$$

$$SD = \sqrt{\frac{\sum X^2}{N} - \frac{(\sum X)^2}{N^2}}$$

$$SD_{pop} = \sqrt{\frac{\sum X^2}{N} - \frac{(\sum X)^2}{N^2}}$$

$$SD_{sample} = \sqrt{\frac{\sum X^2 - (\sum X)^2/N}{N-1}}$$

MEAN, MEDIAN, SD, AND SKEW

A basic underlying assumption of many of the advanced statistical analyses we will do later in the semester is that the data must follow a normal distrubution. What is normal?

$$sk = \frac{3(M - MDN)}{SD}$$

Homework:

1. On the computer, please calculate Mean and standard deviation of our class ages.

2. With the information you have generated from question 1, determine whether or not the distribution of ages is skewed? (Show your calculations and describe the distribution in two sentences or less.)

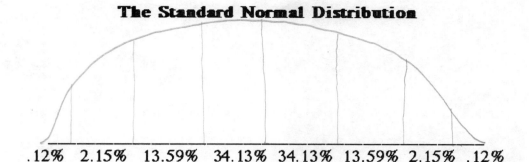

.12%   2.15%   13.59%   34.13%   34.13%   13.59%   2.15%   .12%

$$68.26\%$$
$$95.44\%$$
$$99.74\%$$
$$99.98\%$$

The concept of standard scores

To interpret a score you need to place it in some position with respect to a collection of scores from some reference group.

formula of Z score

$$Z = \frac{X - M}{sd} \quad \text{Thus....} \quad \sum Z = 0 \text{ and } \bar{Z} = \frac{\sum Z}{n} = 0$$

$$T = (100)\left(\frac{X - M}{sd}\right) + 500 \quad \text{or} \quad 500 + 100Z$$

use this formula

T-distribution mean = 500 SD = 100

	M	+1sd	+2sd
	Z=0	Z=1	Z=2
	T=50	T=60	T=70
	GRE=500	GRE=600	GRE=700

Tscore 300 400 500 600 700 800

50 55 60 65

mean 50 SD 5 on this example

65 −50 mean / 15

z Table

(A) z	(B) area between mean and z	(C) area beyond z	(A) z	(B) area between mean and z	(C) area beyond z	(A) z	(B) area between mean and z	(C) area beyond z	(A) z	(B) area between mean and z	(C) area beyond z
0.00	.0000	.5000	0.55	.2088	.2912	1.10	.3643	.1357	1.65	.4505	.0495
0.01	.0040	.4960	0.56	.2123	.2877	1.11	.3665	.1335	1.66	.4515	.0485
0.02	.0080	.4920	0.57	.2157	.2843	1.12	.3686	.1314	1.67	.4525	.0475
0.03	.0120	.4880	0.58	.2190	.2810	1.13	.3708	.1292	1.68	.4535	.0465
0.04	.0160	.4840	0.59	.2224	.2776	1.14	.3729	.1271	1.69	.4545	.0455
0.05	.0199	.4801	0.60	.2257	.2743	1.15	.3749	.1251	1.70	.4554	.0446
0.06	.0239	.4761	0.61	.2291	.2709	1.16	.3770	.1230	1.71	.4564	.0436
0.07	.0279	.4721	0.62	.2324	.2676	1.17	.3790	.1210	1.72	.4573	.0427
0.08	.0319	.4681	0.63	.2357	.2643	1.18	.3810	.1190	1.73	.4582	.0418
0.09	.0359	.4641	0.64	.2389	.2611	1.19	.3830	.1170	1.74	.4591	.0409
0.10	.0398	.4602	0.65	.2422	.2578	1.20	.3849	.1151	1.75	.4599	.0401
0.11	.0438	.4562	0.66	.2454	.2546	1.21	.3869	.1131	1.76	.4608	.0392
0.12	.0478	.4522	0.67	.2486	.2514	1.22	.3888	.1112	1.77	.4616	.0384
0.13	.0517	.4483	0.68	.2517	.2483	1.23	.3907	.1093	1.78	.4625	.0375
0.14	.0557	.4443	0.69	.2549	.2451	1.24	.3925	.1075	1.79	.4633	.0367
0.15	.0596	.4404	0.70	.2580	.2420	1.25	.3944	.1056	1.80	.4641	.0359
0.16	.0636	.4364	0.71	.2611	.2389	1.26	.3962	.1038	1.81	.4649	.0351
0.17	.0675	.4325	0.72	.2642	.2358	1.27	.3980	.1020	1.82	.4656	.0344
0.18	.0714	.4286	0.73	.2673	.2327	1.28	.3997	.1003	1.83	.4664	.0336
0.19	.0753	.4247	0.74	.2704	.2296	1.29	.4015	.0985	1.84	.4671	.0329
0.20	.0793	.4207	0.75	.2734	.2266	1.30	.4032	.0968	1.85	.4678	.0322
0.21	.0832	.4168	0.76	.2764	.2236	1.31	.4049	.0951	1.86	.4686	.0314
0.22	.0871	.4129	0.77	.2794	.2206	1.32	.4066	.0934	1.87	.4693	.0307
0.23	.0910	.4090	0.78	.2823	.2177	1.33	.4082	.0918	1.88	.4699	.0301
0.24	.0948	.4052	0.79	.2852	.2148	1.34	.4099	.0901	1.89	.4706	.0294
0.25	.0987	.4013	0.80	.2881	.2119	1.35	.4115	.0885	1.90	.4713	.0287
0.26	.1026	.3974	0.81	.2910	.2090	1.36	.4131	.0869	1.91	.4719	.0281
0.27	.1064	.3936	0.82	.2939	.2061	1.37	.4147	.0853	1.92	.4726	.0274
0.28	.1103	.3897	0.83	.2967	.2033	1.38	.4162	.0838	1.93	.4732	.0268
0.29	.1141	.3859	0.84	.2995	.2005	1.39	.4177	.0823	1.94	.4738	.0262
0.30	.1179	.3821	0.85	.3023	.1977	1.40	.4192	.0808	1.95	.4744	.0256
0.31	.1217	.3783	0.86	.3051	.1949	1.41	.4207	.0793	1.96	.4750	.0250
0.32	.1255	.3745	0.87	.3078	.1922	1.42	.4222	.0778	1.97	.4756	.0244
0.33	.1293	.3707	0.88	.3106	.1894	1.43	.4236	.0764	1.98	.4761	.0239
0.34	.1331	.3669	0.89	.3133	.1867	1.44	.4251	.0749	1.99	.4767	.0233
0.35	.1368	.3632	0.90	.3159	.1841	1.45	.4265	.0735	2.00	.4772	.0228
0.36	.1406	.3594	0.91	.3186	.1814	1.46	.4279	.0721	2.01	.4778	.0222
0.37	.1443	.3557	0.92	.3212	.1788	1.47	.4292	.0708	2.02	.4783	.0217
0.38	.1480	.3520	0.93	.3238	.1762	1.48	.4306	.0694	2.03	.4788	.0212
0.39	.1517	.3483	0.94	.3264	.1736	1.49	.4319	.0681	2.04	.4793	.0207
0.40	.1554	.3446	0.95	.3289	.1711	1.50	.4332	.0668	2.05	.4798	.0202
0.41	.1591	.3409	0.96	.3315	.1685	1.51	.4345	.0655	2.06	.4803	.0197
0.42	.1628	.3372	0.97	.3340	.1660	1.52	.4357	.0643	2.07	.4808	.0192
0.43	.1664	.3336	0.98	.3365	.1635	1.53	.4370	.0630	2.08	.4812	.0188
0.44	.1700	.3300	0.99	.3389	.1611	1.54	.4382	.0618	2.09	.4817	.0183
0.45	.1736	.3264	1.00	.3413	.1587	1.55	.4394	.0606	2.10	.4821	.0179
0.46	.1772	.3228	1.01	.3438	.1562	1.56	.4406	.0594	2.11	.4826	.0174
0.47	.1808	.3192	1.02	.3461	.1539	1.57	.4418	.0582	2.12	.4830	.0170
0.48	.1844	.3156	1.03	.3485	.1515	1.58	.4429	.0571	2.13	.4834	.0166
0.49	.1879	.3121	1.04	.3508	.1492	1.59	.4441	.0559	2.14	.4838	.0162
0.50	.1915	.3085	1.05	.3531	.1469	1.60	.4452	.0548	2.15	.4842	.0158
0.51	.1950	.3050	1.06	.3554	.1446	1.61	.4463	.0537	2.16	.4846	.0154
0.52	.1985	.3015	1.07	.3577	.1423	1.62	.4474	.0526	2.17	.4850	.0150
0.53	.2019	.2981	1.08	.3599	.1401	1.63	.4484	.0516	2.18	.4854	.0146
0.54	.2054	.2946	1.09	.3621	.1379	1.64	.4495	.0505	2.19	.4857	.0143
									2.20	.4861	.0139
									2.21	.4864	.0136

(A) z	(B) area between mean and z	(C) area beyond z	(A) z	(B) area between mean and z	(C) area beyond z
2.22	.4868	.0132	2.79	.4974	.0026
2.23	.4871	.0129	2.80	.4974	.0026
2.24	.4875	.0125	2.81	.4975	.0025
2.25	.4878	.0122	2.82	.4976	.0024
2.26	.4881	.0119	2.83	.4977	.0023
2.27	.4884	.0116	2.84	.4977	.0023
2.28	.4887	.0113	2.85	.4978	.0022
2.29	.4890	.0110	2.86	.4979	.0021
2.30	.4893	.0107	2.87	.4979	.0021
2.31	.4896	.0104	2.88	.4980	.0020
2.32	.4898	.0102	2.89	.4981	.0019
2.33	.4901	.0099	2.90	.4981	.0019
2.34	.4904	.0096	2.91	.4982	.0018
2.35	.4906	.0094	2.92	.4982	.0018
2.36	.4909	.0091	2.93	.4983	.0017
2.37	.4911	.0089	2.94	.4984	.0016
2.38	.4913	.0087	2.95	.4984	.0016
2.39	.4916	.0084	2.96	.4985	.0015
2.40	.4918	.0082	2.97	.4985	.0015
2.41	.4920	.0080	2.98	.4986	.0014
2.42	.4922	.0078	2.99	.4986	.0014
2.43	.4925	.0075	3.00	.4987	.0013
2.44	.4927	.0073	3.01	.4987	.0013
2.45	.4929	.0071	3.02	.4987	.0013
2.46	.4931	.0069	3.03	.4988	.0012
2.47	.4932	.0068	3.04	.4988	.0012
2.48	.4934	.0066	3.05	.4989	.0011
2.49	.4936	.0064	3.06	.4989	.0011
2.50	.4938	.0062	3.07	.4989	.0011
2.51	.4940	.0060	3.08	.4990	.0010
2.52	.4941	.0059	3.09	.4990	.0010
2.53	.4943	.0057	3.10	.4990	.0010
2.54	.4945	.0055	3.11	.4991	.0009
2.55	.4946	.0054	3.12	.4991	.0009
2.56	.4948	.0052	3.13	.4991	.0009
2.57	.4949	.0051	3.14	.4992	.0008
2.58	.4951	.0049	3.15	.4992	.0008
2.59	.4952	.0048	3.16	.4992	.0008
2.60	.4953	.0047	3.17	.4992	.0008
2.61	.4955	.0045	3.18	.4993	.0007
2.62	.4956	.0044	3.19	.4993	.0007
2.63	.4957	.0043	3.20	.4993	.0007
2.64	.4959	.0041	3.21	.4993	.0007
2.65	.4960	.0040	3.22	.4994	.0006
2.66	.4961	.0039	3.23	.4994	.0006
2.67	.4962	.0038	3.24	.4994	.0006
2.68	.4963	.0037	3.25	.4994	.0006
2.69	.4964	.0036	3.30	.4995	.0005
2.70	.4965	.0035	3.35	.4996	.0004
2.71	.4966	.0034	3.40	.4997	.0003
2.72	.4967	.0033	3.45	.4997	.0003
2.73	.4968	.0032	3.50	.4998	.0002
2.74	.4969	.0031	3.60	.4998	.0002
2.75	.4970	.0030	3.70	.4999	.0001
2.76	.4971	.0029	3.80	.4999	.0001
2.77	.4972	.0028	3.90	.49995	.00005
2.78	.4973	.0027	4.00	.49997	.00003

Normal Curve Homework

1. Given a normal distribution with M of 25 and a SD of 10, find the standard score equivalent for the following scores:

   a. 30   b. 12

2. Find the proportion of area under the normal curve between the mean and the following z-scores

   a. -1.50   b. +2.58   c. +0.15

3. In a normal distribution of M = 50 and SD = 7:

   a. what is the score at the 75th percentile? _____
   b. find the percent of cases scoring above 55 _____
   c. between what scores do the middle 25% of the cases lie? _____
   d. beyond what scores do the most extreme 5% lie? _____

Use the following data to answer questions 4-7. With regard to resting pulse rates: M = 70, SD = 12.

4. What is the probability that, a person chosen at random, would have a resting pulse rate outside 39.04 or 100.96?

5. What is the probability that, a person chosen at random, would have a resting pulse rate less than 39.04?

6. What is the probability that, a person chosen at random, would have a resting pulse rate less than 46.48?

7. What is the probability that, a person chosen at random, would have a resting pulse outside 46.48 or 93.52?

coefficient of determination tells strength of relationship

[r^2 is the coefficient of determination is the amount of variability (predictor) one variable when you know the variability of the other variable]

This is found under the "Regression" menu / "Anova" table

r: height/weight W95

CORRELATION

Correlation: how two variables relate to each other.

Assumptions:
- Both must ber interval or ordinal in nature
- assume both follow a normal curve
- relationship between the 2 variables will be linear
- homoscedasicity

r (relationship)   direction is either + or -
                   magnitude 0.0 to -0.0

Definitions:

Correlation = relationship between 2 variables

Correlation coefficient = a measure that expresses the extent to which 2 variables are related.

Positive relationship = variables are said to be positively related when a high score on one is accompanied by a high score on the other. Conversely, low scores on one variable are associated with low scores on the other.

Negative relationship = variables are said to be negatively related when a high score on one is accompanied by a low score on the other. Conversely, low scores on one variable are associated with high scores on the other.

Scatter diagram = a graphic device employed to represent the variation in 2 variables.

Pearson Product Moment Correlation (r) *(raw score formula) takes 5 columns*

raw score method for calculating correlation coefficients

use this one

$$r = \frac{n\sum XY - (\sum X)(\sum Y)}{\sqrt{[n\sum X^2 - (\sum X)^2][n\sum Y^2 - (\sum Y)^2]}}$$

(only interval data)

The **sum of squares** (mean deviation) method to calculate Pearson r

$$r = \frac{\sum (X - \bar{X})(Y - \bar{Y})}{\sqrt{(SSx)(SSy)}}$$

don't use this one

Spearman Correlation
is found under the "Statistics"
menu / "Spearman Correlation"
r_s = height/weight W95

SPEARMAN r (r_s or rank correlation coefficient) is a correlation coefficient employed with ordering (ranked) data. *(only ordinal data)*

$$r_s = 1 - \left(\frac{6 \Sigma D2}{N(N^2 - 1)} \right)$$

REGRESSION AND PREDICTION

The beauty of correlated data, particularly when the correlation is high (such as in the case of weight of the auto and miles per gallon used), is that we can predict values of one variable from knowledge of the other.

The method is known as regression analysis.

X' and Y', X prime and Y prime means X-predicted and Y-predicted or estimated X and Y.

$$Y' = \bar{Y} + r\frac{s_y}{s_x}(X - \bar{X})$$

$$X' = \bar{X} + r\frac{s_x}{s_y}(Y - \bar{Y})$$

CONSTRUCTING REGRESSION LINES

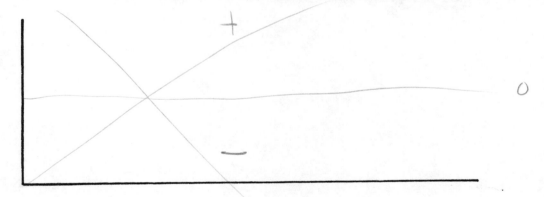

STANDARD ERROR OF ESTIMATE AROUND THE REGRESSION LINE

The standard error of estimate (the same) is the standard deviation of scores around the regression line.

$$s_{est\ y} = s_y \sqrt{\frac{N(1 - r^2)}{N - 2}}$$

$$s_{est\ x} = s_x \sqrt{\frac{N(1 - r^2)}{N - 2}}$$

Pretest 2 Worksheet:

(To earn credit, describe how you arrived at the correct answer.)

1. Given a normal distribution with M of 25 and a SD of 10, find the z-score equivalent for the following scores:

   a. 30   b. 12

   a. .5
   b. -1.3

   use formulas on p. 29

2. Find the proportion of area under the normal curve between the mean and the following z-scores

   a. -1.50   b. +2.58   c. +0.15

   a. .4332
   b. .4951
   c. .0596

3. For question #2, transform the z-scores given into T-scores.

   a. 350   b. 758   c. 515

4. In a T-score distribution the mean is equal to __500__ and the standard deviation is equal to __100__.

5. In a normal distribution of M = 50 and SD = 7:
   a. what is the score at the 75th percentile? __54.76__
   b. find the percent of cases scoring above 55 __23.89__
   c. between what scores do the middle 25% of the cases lie? __47.76 - 52.24__
   d. beyond what scores do the most extreme 5% lie? __36.28 - 63.72__

   2½ - 97½

   # finds z score deals w/ formula

6. Calculate the Pearson r for the following scores: r = +.724

#	Score 1	x^2	Score 2	y^2	$x \cdot y$
1	160	25600	2.59	6.7081	414.4
2	100	10000	1.00	1.00	100
3	140	19600	0.90	.81	126
4	120	14400	1.50	2.25	180
5	90	8100	0.95	.9025	85.5

   $\Sigma x = 610$ $\Sigma x^2 = 77700$ $\Sigma y = 6.94$ $\Sigma y^2 = 11.6706$ $\Sigma x \cdot y = 905.9$

   N = 5

   $r = \dfrac{n\Sigma xy - (\Sigma x)(\Sigma y)}{\sqrt{[n\Sigma x^2 - (\Sigma x)^2][n\Sigma y^2 - (\Sigma y)^2]}}$

   $r = \dfrac{5(905.9) - (610)(6.94)}{\sqrt{[388500 - 372100][58.353 - 48.16]}}$

   $r = \dfrac{4529.5 - 4233.4}{\sqrt{(16400)\, 10.1894}}$

   $r = \dfrac{296.1}{408.7862}$

   r = 7.24

$r_s = 1 - \left(\dfrac{6 \Sigma D^2}{N(N^2-1)}\right)$

7. Calculate a Spearman r (r_s) for the following ranked ratings: $r_s = .68$ $r_s = 1 - \dfrac{108}{7(48)}$

#	N=7	Rank 1	Rank 2	D	D²
a		1	3	-2	4
b		2	1	1	1
c		3	4	-1	1
d		4	5	-1	1
e		5	2	3	9
f		6	7	-1	1
g		7	6	1	1

$\Sigma D^2 = 18$

$r_s = 1 - \dfrac{108}{336}$

$r_s = 1 - .32$

$\boxed{r_s = .68}$

8. With regard to the following data, conduct the necessary calculations:
   x-variable   y-variable   r = 0.45   N = 50
   M = 38   M = 1.90
   SD = 8   SD = 0.40

   a. given a score of 44 on the X-variable what is Y'? __2.035__

   b. determine the standard error of Y. __.364__

   c. Discuss the meaning of the answer to b. above. The predicted value of y is 2.035 + or -.36

$y' = \bar{Y} + r \dfrac{S_y}{S_x}(X - \bar{X})$

$y' = 1.90 + .45\left(\dfrac{.40}{8}\right)(44 - 38)$

$y' = 1.90 + .45(.05)(6)$

$y' = 1.90 + .0225(6)$

$y' = 1.90 + .135$

$y' = 2.035$

$S_{est\,y} = S_y \sqrt{\dfrac{N(1-r^2)}{N-2}}$

$= .40 \sqrt{\dfrac{50(1 - .2025)}{48}}$

$= .40 \sqrt{\dfrac{50(.7975)}{48}}$

$= .40 \sqrt{\dfrac{39.875}{48}}$

$= .40 \sqrt{.8307}$

$= .40 (.91)$

$S_{est\,y} = .364$

STATISTICAL INFERENCE

1. **Why statistical inference?**

2. **The concept of Sampling Distributions**

3. **Significance Levels**

4. **Hypotheses**

    Null Hypothesis (H_0)

    Alternate Hypothesis (H_1)

        Directional hypothesis

        Nondirectional hypothesis

5. **Statistical Error** (Type I, Alpha & Type II, Beta)

    When we reject the null hypothesis and it is really true, it is called a Type I error.

    A Type II error is when we fail to reject the null hypothesis when it is actually false.

sigma — standard deviation of a population

$$\sigma_{\bar{x}} = \frac{\sigma}{\sqrt{N}}$$ (standard error of the mean) (# in sample)

$$Z = \frac{\bar{x} - \mu}{\sigma_{\bar{x}}}$$ population mean — μ (mu)

$$t = \frac{\bar{x} - \mu}{S_{\bar{x}}}$$

standard deviation of a sample

$$S_{\bar{x}} = \frac{S}{\sqrt{N-1}}$$

if computed T is $\geq$ the chart critical value then there is a sign. diff. reject H_0

if T is $<$ the chart crit. value then we do not reject H_0

n = sample size

Student's t-tests

A statistician named William Gosset published under the name Student is responsible for describing a family of distributions that permits the testing of hypotheses about samples drawn from normally distributed populations. These distributions are known as t-distributions or Student's t.

The questions we will answer using the student's t statistic include:

1. How does the mean for a sample compare with the mean of a population? In other words, is the sample drawn from the population? Is the sample different from the population? (Do females in this class differ significantly from females in the population in terms of IQ?)

2. How does two different samples compare with each other? (Are males and females different in their appreciation for art?)

3. How does some interaction effect one sample? (Does some drug therapy impact on some disease?)

In all three cases, we are looking at the disparity in mean scores.

σ = sigma   *μ = mu*

The standard error of the mean is defined as the theoretical standard deviation of sample means, of a given sample drawn from a population.

$$\sigma_{\bar{X}} = \frac{\sigma}{\sqrt{N}}$$

$$Z = \frac{\bar{X} - \mu}{\sigma_{\bar{X}}}$$

Student's t-ratio: One case t. (Comparing sample mean to population mean.)

The formula is as follows: $t = \dfrac{\bar{X} - \mu_0}{s_{\bar{X}}}$

S = standard deviation

(standard error of mean when you do not know the standard error of the mean)

$$s_{\bar{X}} = \frac{s}{\sqrt{N-1}} \text{ —sample}$$

where:
- t = the t-ratio
- X = sample mean
- μ = population mean
- df = N-1
- $S_{\bar{X}}$ = standard error of the mean = $\dfrac{s}{\sqrt{n-1}}$

get T value go to sign level if sign level is greater than T

independent sample
steps 1-6 are same
#7.

$$S_{\bar{X}_1-\bar{X}_2} = \sqrt{\left(\frac{40.1+30}{10+8-2}\right)\left(\frac{1}{10}+\frac{1}{8}\right)}$$

$$\sqrt{\left(\frac{70.1}{16}\right)(.1+.125)}$$

$$\sqrt{(4.38)(.225)}$$

$$\sqrt{.985}$$

$$S_{\bar{X}_1-\bar{X}_2} = .99$$

$$t = \frac{(3.3-2.5)}{.99}$$

$$t = .808$$

$$149 - \frac{(33)^2}{10} \overset{SS_1}{=} 40.1$$

$$80 - \frac{(20)^2}{8} \overset{SS_2}{=} 30$$

Student's t: 2 independent samples

You use the Student's t ratio for analyses that compare two groups that are independent.

In a 2-sample analysis, we are drawing 2 samples, finding the differences between the means of each pair, and obtaining a distribution of these differences.

We are attempting to answer the question "does these two samples appear to be drawn from the same population? Is there enough disparity between their means to indicate that they are dissimilar?"

The assumptions for the 2 sample Student's t are:
1. the samples must be interval data.
2. the samples must follow a normal curve
3. homogeneity of variance.

— one case t — one sample T

Remember that the **standard error of the mean** is defined as the theoretical standard deviation of sample means, of a given sample drawn from a population.

In the 2 sample case we are looking at the **standard error of the** *2 sample T* **differences between the means**. This is defined as the standard deviation of the sampling distribution of the difference between the means.

The standard error of the difference between the mean is calculated using the following formula: *second*

$$s_{\bar{X}_1 - \bar{X}_2} = \sqrt{\left(\frac{SS_1 + SS_2}{N_1 + N_2 - 2}\right)\left(\frac{1}{N_1} + \frac{1}{N_2}\right)}$$

formula for indep. sample

However, if $N_1 = N_2 = N$, Formula (13.1) simplifies to

$$s_{\bar{X}_1 - \bar{X}_2} = \sqrt{\frac{SS_1 + SS_2}{N(N-1)}}$$

where: *first*

$$SS_1 = \sum X_1^2 - \frac{(\sum X_1)^2}{N_1} \quad \text{and} \quad SS_2 = \sum X_2^2 - \frac{(\sum X_2)^2}{N_2}$$

The t-ratio formula is a follows:

this is one to use last *third* — *don't need*

$$t = \frac{(\bar{X}_1 - \bar{X}_2) - (\mu_1 - \mu_2)}{s_{\bar{X}_1 - \bar{X}_2}}$$

need df

Student's t-Ratio for Matched paired samples

We are often looking at a pre- post-design in which we are looking at a single group before and after some intervention.

We can also look at differences in matched samples.

Student's t for matched pairs = between 2 *s* *third difference*

$$t = \frac{\bar{D} - \mu_{\bar{D}}}{s_{\bar{D}}} = \frac{\bar{D}}{s_{\bar{D}}}$$

($\mu_{\bar{D}} = 0$)

$\bar{D}$ $\bar{D}^2$

where: the standard error of the mean difference is

second
$$s_{\bar{D}} = \sqrt{\frac{SS_D}{N(N-1)}}$$

$$t = \frac{6.29}{2.51}$$

$$t = 2.50$$

and: $SS_D =$

first
$$SS_D = \sum D^2 - \frac{(\sum D)^2}{N}$$

$$542 - \frac{1936}{7}$$

$$SS_D = 542 - 276.57$$

$$SS_D = 265.43$$

$$s_{\bar{D}} = \sqrt{\frac{265.4}{7(7-1)}}$$

$$s_{\bar{D}} = \sqrt{\frac{265.4}{42}}$$

$$\sqrt{6.3}$$

$$s_{\bar{D}} = 2.51$$

degrees of freedom - allows you to hedge for error

5'9" (average height for males)   5'8", 5'10", 5'10" — 3 degrees of freedom

the smaller the distribution — the more it looks abnormal

a negative t means the second group (μ) is larger than the first group $(\bar{X})$

$$t = \frac{\bar{X} - \mu}{S_{\bar{X}}}$$

$$S_{\bar{X}} = \frac{S}{\sqrt{N-1}}$$

$$S_{\bar{X}} = \frac{3.95}{\sqrt{50-1}}$$

$$S_{\bar{X}} = \frac{3.95}{\sqrt{49}}$$

$$S_{\bar{X}} = .56428$$

Critical Values of *t*

For any given df, the table shows the values of *t* corresponding to various levels of probability. The obtained *t* is significant at a given level if it is equal to or *greater than* the value shown in the table.

df	Level of significance for one-tailed test					
	.10	.05	.025	.01	.005	.0005
	Level of significance for two-tailed test					
	.20	.10	.05	.02	.01	.001
1	3.078	6.314	12.706	31.821	63.657	636.619
2	1.886	2.920	4.303	6.965	9.925	31.598
3	1.638	2.353	3.182	4.541	5.841	12.941
4	1.533	2.132	2.776	3.747	4.604	8.610
5	1.476	2.015	2.571	3.365	4.032	6.859
6	1.440	1.943	2.447	3.143	3.707	5.959
7	1.415	1.895	2.365	2.998	3.499	5.405
8	1.397	1.860	2.306	2.896	3.355	5.041
9	1.383	1.833	2.262	2.821	3.250	4.781
10	1.372	1.812	2.228	2.764	3.169	4.587
11	1.363	1.796	2.201	2.718	3.106	4.437
12	1.356	1.782	2.179	2.681	3.055	4.318
13	1.350	1.771	2.160	2.650	3.012	4.221
14	1.345	1.761	2.145	2.624	2.977	4.140
15	1.341	1.753	2.131	2.602	2.947	4.073
16	1.337	1.746	2.120	2.583	2.921	4.015
17	1.333	1.740	2.110	2.567	2.898	3.965
18	1.330	1.734	2.101	2.552	2.878	3.922
19	1.328	1.729	2.093	2.539	2.861	3.883
20	1.325	1.725	2.086	2.528	2.845	3.850
21	1.323	1.721	2.080	2.518	2.831	3.819
22	1.321	1.717	2.074	2.508	2.819	3.792
23	1.319	1.714	2.069	2.500	2.807	3.767
24	1.318	1.711	2.064	2.492	2.797	3.745
25	1.316	1.708	2.060	2.485	2.787	3.725
26	1.315	1.706	2.056	2.479	2.779	3.707
27	1.314	1.703	2.052	2.473	2.771	3.690
28	1.313	1.701	2.048	2.467	2.763	3.674
29	1.311	1.699	2.045	2.462	2.756	3.659
30	1.310	1.697	2.042	2.457	2.750	3.646
40	1.303	1.684	2.021	2.423	2.704	3.551
60	1.296	1.671	2.000	2.390	2.660	3.460
120	1.289	1.658	1.980	2.358	2.617	3.373
∞	1.282	1.645	1.960	2.326	2.576	3.291

same as normal distribution

A University Worksite Health Promotion and Wellness Education Program Model

Parris R. Watts, Alex Waigandt, Ben R. Londeree and Michelle Sappington

Abstract

During the 1980s, worksite health promotion and wellness education programs became increasingly prevalent in business and industry. A similar pattern currently is emerging among institutions of higher education. To assist in development of college and university programs, this article presents philosophy, delineates goals and objectives, and describes interventions applied and components included within the Missouri University Health Education and Lifestyle Promotion (H.E.L.P.) Program. Unlike most other college and university wellness efforts, the MU H.E.L.P. Program utilizes a carefully structured, "comprehensive package" approach. This article emphasizes benefits of networking existing campus resources and personnel and the importance of effective program design, implementation, and evaluation. The MU H.E.L.P. Program serves as an excellent example of how a multidisciplinary approach to employee health promotion and wellness education programming can be cost-effective, time-efficient, and highly successful in a higher education setting. Documentation of the program's success is presented. Statistically significant improvements in seven selected variables between repeated assessment measures were found. These results are consistent with those reported in research conducted within business and industrial settings.

Parris R. Watts is an associate professor of health education and Director of the Missouri University H.E.L.P. Program, Department of Health and Physical Education, Missouri University, Columbia, MO 65211. Alex Waigandt is an associate professor of health education and Director of the Health Education Program, Department of Health and Physical Education, Missouri University. Ben R. Londeree is an associate professor of physical education and Director of the Human Performance Laboratory, Department of Health and Physical Education, Missouri University. Michelle Sappington is a graduate student in the Department of Health and Physical Education, Missouri University.

Worksite health promotion and wellness education programs have became more prevalent in business and industry in recent years (Reed et al., 1986; Chen, 1988; Fielding & Piserchia, 1989; Gebhardt & Crump, 1990; Green & Kreuter, 1990). A variety of behaviorally oriented interventions including nutrition education, weight control, exercise, smoking cessation, and stress management typically have been offered in these programs (Pauly et al., 1982; Bernacki & Baun, 1984; Blair et al., 1986; Bly et al., 1986; Baun & Bernacki, 1986; Rudman & Steinhardt, 1988; Breslow et al., 1990; Eddy et al., 1990). College and university health promotion and wellness education efforts have begun to evolve along with corporate programs and they appear to be on the increase (Parsons, 1987). Campus programs have been developed to enhance faculty and staff health status, using educational and behavioral modification strategies similar to those previously adopted by business and industry (Seaward & Snelling, 1990).

Commonly, college and university employee worksite health promotion and wellness education programs use a "cafeteria style" approach. This program design offers numerous health related interventions to faculty and staff and each employee selects one or more within which to become involved. Various forms of physical activity from walking to water aerobics, from jogging to cycling, from aerobic dance to using stairclimbing equipment, and from racquet sports to working out on a Nordic Track ordinarily are included. Nutrition education classes usually are provided, wherein emphasis is placed on weight loss and healthful eating habits. Stress management frequently is included, as are smoking cessation interventions.

During 1988 and 1989, the primary author of this article visited the campuses of several of America's leading college and university employee wellness programs. As a result of those visits, it was decided that the emerging Missouri University program would be designed using a carefully structured, "comprehensive package" approach. The comprehensive package differs from the cafeteria style approach in that participants are in-

volved in all interventions included in the program. The purpose of this article is to provide an overview of the Missouri University employee wellness model, known as the Health Education and Lifestyle Promotion (H.E.L.P.) Program.

Program Philosophy

Girdano (1986) has stated that essential to development of a quality health promotion and wellness education program is establishment of a solid philosophical foundation. The philosophy should consider the nature of health promotion and wellness education and health behavior change. It also should take into consideration the needs of program participants.

The philosophical foundation upon which the Missouri University H.E.L.P. Program has been built is known as the Health for Human Wholeness Model (Figure 1). The model clearly depicts the need to address all dimensions of the participants' lives, in a well-balanced approach. Within the context of the H.E.L.P. Program, health is defined as a quality of life, involving the dynamic interaction and interdependency of all six life dimensions of the whole human being. Human wholeness is perceived as becoming the best one can become, in spite of and even in light of the individual's limitations in the six life dimensions.

Impacting those life dimensions are four major determinants of health: heredity, medical care, environment, and lifestyle. Although H.E.L.P. Program participants are caused to recognize the importance of all determinants of health, they are taught that lifestyle potentially affects their own personal health more than the other three factors combined (Girdano, 1986). With that concept in mind, participants are enabled to realize that they possess an internal locus of control over their health related decisions and behaviors, and as a result, they essentially hold their personal health destinies in their own hands.

Missouri University employees involved in the H.E.L.P. Program are instructed regarding the need to assume responsibility for their personal health choices. However, a critical point must be interjected here. Assumption of personal health responsibility evolves gradually throughout the course of the program. Initially, the responsibility is shared by the participating group of faculty and staff. Then, over a period of time, and within a family type of supportive structure, individuals systematically assume increasing amounts of personal responsibility for their health related decisions and behaviors. Such an approach does not overwhelm the participants with more than they realistically can handle as they begin the process of improving the quality of their lives through their involvement in the H.E.L.P. Program.

Program Goals and Objectives

Also known as outcomes, health promotion and wellness education goals and objectives form

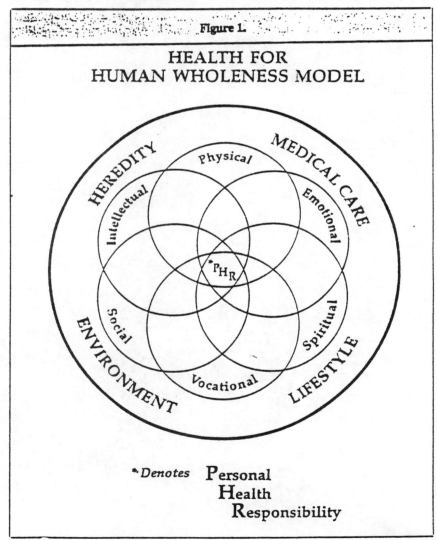

Figure 1.

HEALTH FOR HUMAN WHOLENESS MODEL

*Denotes Personal Health Responsibility

Figure 2. Missouri University Health Education and Lifestyle Promotion (H.E.L.P.) Program Hierarchy of Programmatic Goals and Objectives

MISSOURI UNIVERSITY
HEALTH EDUCATION AND LIFESTYLE PROMOTION (H.E.L.P.) PROGRAM

HIERARCHY OF PROGRAMATIC GOALS AND OBJECTIVES

GOAL

Improved levels of the physical, intellectual, emotional, social, spiritual, and vocational dimensions of health experienced by H.E.L.P. Program Participants, as a result of health-related knowledge acquired, attitudes changed, and behaviors modified in all six dimensions of their lives

PRIMARY SUB-GOAL	SECONDARY SUB-GOAL
Establishment and/or reinforcement of health promotion influences in the lives of responsive MU faculty and staff	Establishment and/or reinforcement of health promotion influences in the lives of responsive non-MU employees who reside in Columbia area

OUTCOME OBJECTIVE

To reduce, over time, health risks associated with the lack of regular aerobic exercise, excessive body fat, improper eating habits, poor stress management practices, and a negative self-image

BEHAVIORAL OBJECTIVES

- To lower resting heart rate
- To lower exercise heart rate
- To lower total cholesterol
- To lower systolic blood pressure
- To lower diastolic blood pressure
- To reduce percentage of body fat
- To increase consumption of complex carbohydrates and dietary fiber
- To reduce consumption of sodium, dietary cholesterol, saturated fat, sugar, and excessive calories
- To improve time management skills
- To identify major stressors in daily life
- To practice relaxation techniques learned

BEHAVIORAL CHANGE INTERVENTIONS

Moderate Exercise
Body Fat Reduction and Management
Dietary Modification
Stress Awareness and Management
Positive Self-Image Enhancement

PRIMARY PROCESS OBJECTIVE	SECONDARY PROCESS OBJECTIVE
Recruiting, educating, motivating, counseling, and encouraging H.E.L.P. Program participants and evaluating their progress	Educating, motivating, counseling, and mentoring H410 and H400 students serving as facilitators in the H.E.L.P. Program and evaluating their performance

the underpinning of the program planning process. According to Girdano (1986), goals and objectives should be formulated on the basis of their potential for: (1) realistic achievement, (2) modification of behaviors, (3) institutional benefit, (4) participant benefit, and (5) measurability. Although good program planning progresses from philosophy through goals and objectives to program interventions and components, the process goes forward and backward, with the end product often justifying the program (Brennan, 1981). Figure 2 provides a summary of the goals and objectives of the H.E.L.P. Program and their relationship to program interventions, components, and measurable variables.

Program Interventions and Components

Health promotion and wellness education program goals and objectives, interventions, and components are all interdependent and intersupportive. Combined, they represent what is wanted and what is realistically feasible within parameters of existing program constraints (Girdano, 1986). Figure 3 presents a schematic overview of the Missouri University H.E.L.P. Program. Beneath the overarching expected outcome of health promotion habit formation, derived from the program goal of improved participant health status, are found the fundamental interventions applied in the program: (1) physical activity, (2) nutrition education, and (3) stress awareness and management. The two additional expected outcomes: (1) assumption of personal health response ability, and (2) enhancement of positive self-image, conceptually complete the program model.

Within each program intervention, there are various components that enable the intervention to have maximal, measurable effects on the participants. As a part of the physical activity intervention, extensive blood chemistry analyses (including lipid profiles) are performed before and after a 15 week exercise regimen is initiated. Data are analyzed to verify reductions in the primary cardiovascular heart disease risk factor of high total cholesterol. The blood tests also screen for a variety of other indicators to identify any conditions which may need medical attention. A thorough assessment of physical fitness is done within the Missouri University Department of Health and Physical Education Human Performance Laboratory before and after the exercise intervention is applied. Assessment results are used to verify improvement in cardiovascular, body fat percentage, and respiratory measurements.

Related to the physical activity intervention, an individualized exercise prescription is prepared for each H.E.L.P. Program participant. This prescription is tailored to personal needs, interests, and capabilities of the participants. The prescription is designed to maximize benefits derived from the exercise intervention and to minimize the risk of injury while exercising. An accompanying body composition analysis provides body fat percentage baseline data upon which to formulate a realistic fat reduction goal and with which to compare at the end of the 15 week program. Muscle balance and posture analyses, and related prescriptions, furnish participants with specific strength and flexibility exercises and other recommendations to correct imbalances discovered during testing.

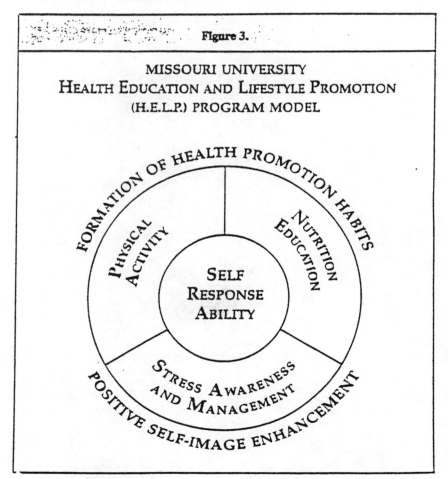

Figure 3.
MISSOURI UNIVERSITY
HEALTH EDUCATION AND LIFESTYLE PROMOTION
(H.E.L.P.) PROGRAM MODEL

A proven and effective aerobic physical activity program, which has been operational for more than 15 years, is the core of the physical activity intervention. The program is administered by exercise physiology graduate students, under the supervision of the Director of the Human Performance Laboratory. Exercise sessions offered Mondays, Wednesdays, and Fridays, before work, after work, and during the noon hour, emphasize proper warm-up techniques, walking, jogging, cycling, exercises with weights, and cool-down activities. The physical activity intervention provides an opportunity for each participant to carry out his or her exercise prescription, based on the previously completed fitness assessment.

The second major H.E.L.P. Program intervention, nutrition education, has three components. Initially, dietary modification prescriptions are prepared for all participants, based on their blood lipid profile results and on an analysis of their personal eating habits. Participants' eating habits are analyzed with use of a food and beverage consumption record they are asked to keep for three consecutive days during the first week of the program. Emphasis is placed on increasing the intake of complex carbohydrates and fiber in the diet and on reducing saturated fat, sodium, dietary cholesterol, and sugar consumption.

Next, body fat reduction and management plans are developed for each participant, using body composition data gathered via hydrostatic weighing, a realistic body fat percentage goal, and recommended healthful dietary changes that are acceptable to the participant. Permanent alterations in personal eating habits are stressed to promote future maintenance of body fat reduction achieved. Finally, a highly informative, time efficient supermarket tour, which emphasizes how to shop for groceries more healthfully and cost effectively, is conducted. Application of the nutrition related label reading skills taught as a part of the nutrition education intervention, is stressed throughout the tour, which is conducted by a nutrition education specialist.

Stress awareness and management comprises the third major H.E.L.P. Program intervention. Stress management techniques, with an emphasis on learning and practicing them, are presented as a part of this intervention. Included is information on time management, stressor identification, and relaxation exercises that can be utilized in a wide variety of settings. Closely associated with the stress awareness and management intervention is a strong emphasis on positive, self-image enhancement. Throughout the full semester H.E.L.P. Program, the positive, reinforcing, and cumulative effects of all three primary interventions and their related components are stressed. These, combined with much personalized attention given by program staff and resource persons and the camaraderie that develops among the group of participants, contribute immensely to enhancement of personal self-image.

Two vital program components that not only span all interventions, but perhaps are the true bricks and mortar of the H.E.L.P. Program, are: (1) the noontime wellness lifestyle course, and (2) involvement of Missouri University graduate students. The Tuesday and Thursday noontime course meets 30 times during the semester for 40 minutes each session. Participants bring and eat their lunches while they are provided with a comprehensive health education experience. The course emphasizes establishing and "rehabiting" positive health practices and covers exercise, dietary modification, body fat management, stress awareness and management, and positive self-image enhancement concepts in considerable detail.

Health education masters and doctoral students who are becoming professionally prepared as health promotion and wellness education specialists are actively involved in the H.E.L.P. Program as consultants and facilitators. Initially within the Health Promotion and Wellness Education course, then later in practicum coursework, students gain valuable experience while monitoring and motivating program participants and in developing new and refining existing program components.

Evaluation of Program Effectiveness

The abundance of literature, some of which was cited previously in this article, regarding benefits of health promotion and wellness education programs in corporate America would seem to be the justification for providing similar programs to faculty and staff on college and university campuses. Despite the fact that research is done inherently at most institutions of higher education, little has been published substantiating the effectiveness of health promotion and wellness education programs for college and

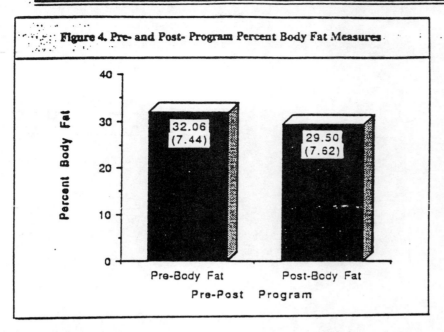

Figure 4. Pre- and Post- Program Percent Body Fat Measures

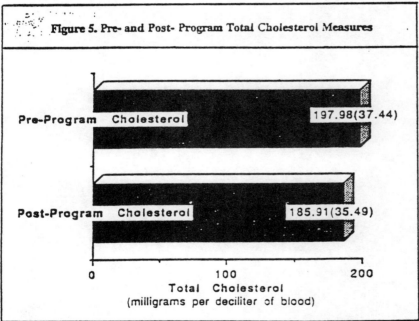

Figure 5. Pre- and Post- Program Total Cholesterol Measures

university employees.

In an attempt to evaluate the status of faculty and staff health promotion programs on university campuses, Parsons (1987) studied 13 midwestern universities offering employee programs. Results indicated that the diversity of the university community directly impacted the organization of university wellness programs. Parsons cited the opportunity for research, availability of student practicum/internship experiences, and potential for external funding as benefits for universities with functioning health promotion and wellness education programs.

Although Parsons (1987) found that many campuses currently are developing and offering wellness programs for their faculty and staff, few have highly structured, comprehensive, combined intervention programs like the Missouri University H.E.L.P. Model. Consequently, little has been published regarding effectiveness of such programs. To demonstrate the positive effect of the MU program and to make a needed contribution to the literature regarding the impact of comprehensive health promotion programs on university employees, results of the initial three semester-long H.E.L.P. sessions will be presented.

All 54 of the participants who completed one of the three program sessions were employed by Missouri University. Twenty of the employees were males, and 34 were females. The average age of males was 41.70 years, and the female mean age was 37.74.

Data analysis results demonstrated that a statistically significant change occurred in the seven physiological variables studied. Table 1 presents these data.

Dry body weight was decreased by an average of more than five and one-half pounds. The mean body fat reduction experienced by H.E.L.P. Program participants was over two and one-half percent (see Figure 4). As shown in Figure 5, average total cholesterol levels of Missouri University faculty and staff dropped by more than 12 milligrams per deciliter of blood. This represents a six percent reduction in the mean total cholesterol level of program participants. According to the American Heart Association, that decrease can be translated into a 12 percent average reduction in coronary heart disease risk among program participants.

The drop in the mean systolic blood pressure of participants was greater than five and one-half millimeters of mercury. This decrease resulted in an average systolic blood pressure which was within the normal

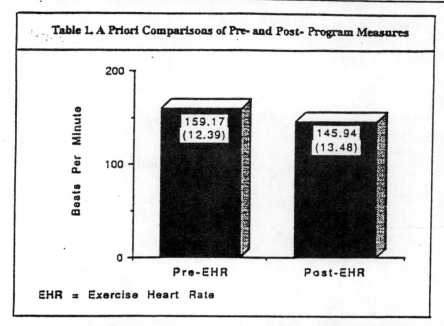

Table 1. A Priori Comparisons of Pre- and Post- Program Measures

EHR = Exercise Heart Rate

range. The mean diastolic blood pressure of MU employees studied was lowered by nearly three and one-half millimeters of mercury. The mean resting heart rate of the subjects was lowered by almost three beats per minute. Even though that decrease may not seem impressive, it represents more than 4,000 heartbeats saved per day per subject. As illustrated in Figure 6, average exercise heart rate measures were reduced by over 13 beats per minute. Undoubtedly this result was related to adoption of a strong work ethic that was observed among participants during the aerobic exercise sessions.

Based on analysis of the data gathered, the following statements regarding the impact of the Missouri University H.E.L.P. Program on participating subjects are presented.

1. Although participant weight loss was not dramatic, it was significant.
2. Significant improvement in body composition occurred among subjects.
3. Total cholesterol levels were lowered significantly and translated into considerable reductions in the participants' coronary heart disease risk.
4. Systolic blood pressure levels dropped significantly during the program, thereby causing them to be in the normal range at the end of the investigation.
5. Although participant diastolic blood pressure measurements were in the normal range at the beginning of

Figure 6. Pre- and Post- Program Exercise Heart Rate Measures

Variable	Pre-measure M(sd)	Post-measure M (sd)	Paired Observations	df	t	significance
Weight	174.93(36.87)	169.30(34.23)	54	53	4.75	.001
Percent Body Fat	32.06(7.44)	29.50(7.62)	54	53	5.60	.001
Total Cholesterol	197.98(37.44)	185.91(35.49)	54	53	3.91	.001
Systolic Blood Pres	122.07(15.97)	116.39(11.92)	54	53	3.77	.001
Diastolic Blood Pres	78.85(10.06)	75.44(9.19)	54	53	3.45	.001
Resting Heart Rate	73.93(7.72)	70.96(9.00)	54	53	2.73	.01
Exercise Heart Rate	159.17(12.39)	145.94(13.48)	54	53	7.97	.001

the study, they were significantly reduced.

6. In spite of being the smallest of the changes in health related variables studied, decreased resting heart rates were beneficial outcomes of the program.

7. Exercise heart rates were lowered significantly, which was consistent with considerable effort expended by subjects during physical activity.

Summary

This article has presented a health promotion and wellness education programmatic model that has worked well at Missouri University. The MU Employee H.E.L.P. Program has utilized already existing exercise and classroom facilities, program components (e.g., the Human Performance Laboratory), personnel (most of whom volunteer their time to provide instructional and other services), and resource materials (e.g., those developed by the Nutrition Extension Office and the Human Resource Development Office, for use in the nutrition education and stress awareness offices, for use in nutrition education and stress awareness and management interventions, respectively).

Because faculty and staff participants pay for services provided ($200 for the entire program, which they consider to be a reasonable amount), the cost of the program to Missouri University is minimal. During the 1990-91 academic year, the only funding that was required to conduct the program was $5,000 to pay partial graduate assistantship stipends for three students and less than an additional $2,000 to provide for their coursework fee waivers. (During the 1988-89 academic year, which was the initial year the program was offered, $1,200 was donated by Lifeplans, Inc., d/b/a/Network Health Systems, and $300 was contributed by the Missouri University School of Health Related Professions to fund a partial graduate assistantship stipend.)

Clearly, the secret to the success of the H.E.L.P. Program, which has been documented in this article, is the willingness of key health related professionals on the MU campus to consolidate their efforts. Such networking has demonstrated to the administration and the faculty and staff, that improving the health status of participating employees is of primary importance to campus personnel who conduct the program. That cooperative spirit, combined with a solid programmatic philosophy, realistic goals and objectives that are measurable, bodes well for the future of the Missouri University Health Education and Lifestyle Promotion Program. Hopefully its programmatic model will be useful to other colleges and universities considering initiation of health promotion and wellness education efforts to benefit their employees and, as a by-product, the institutions themselves.

Baun, W. B., Bernacki, E. J., & Tsai, S. P. (1986). A preliminary investigation: Effect of a corporate fitness program on absenteeism and health care cost. *Journal of Occupational Medicine, 28,* 18-22.

Bernacki, E. J., & Baun, W. B. (1984). The relationship of job performance to exercise adherence in a corporate fitness program. *Journal of Occupational Medicine, 26,* 529-531.

Blair, S. N., Piserchia, P. V., & Wilbur, C. S. (1986). A public health intervention model for worksite health promotion: Impact of exercise and physical fitness in a health promotion plan after 24 months. *Journal of the American Medical Association, 255,* 921-926.

Bly, J., Jones, R., & Richardson, T. (1986). Impact of worksite health promotion on health care costs and utilization: Evaluation of Johnson and Johnson's live for life program. *Journal of the American Medical Association, 256,* 3235-3240.

Breslow, L., Fielding, J., Herrman, A. A., & Wilbur, C. S. (1990). Worksite health promotion: Its evolution and the Johnson & Johnson experience. *Preventive Medicine, 19,* 13-21.

Chen, M. S. (1988). Wellness in the workplace: Beyond the point of no return. *Health Values: Achieving High Level Wellness, 12,* 16-22.

Eddy, J. M., Eynon, D., Nagy, S., & Paradossi, P. J. (1990). Impact of a physical fitness program in a blue-collar workforce. *Health Values: Health Behavior, Education and Promotion, 14*(6), 14-23.

Fielding, J. E., & Piserchia, P. V. (1989). Frequency of worksite health promotion activities. *American Journal of Public Health, 79,* 16-20.

Gebhardt, D. L., & Crump, C. E. (1990). Employee fitness and wellness programs in the workplace. *American Psychologist, 45,* 262-272.

Girdano, D. A. (1986). *Occupational health promotion: A practical guide to program development.* New York: Macmillan Publishing Co.

Green, L. W., & Kreuter, M. W. (1990). Health promotion as a public health strategy for the 1990s. *Annual Review of Public Health, 11,* 319-324.

Parsons, T. W. (1987). Faculty/staff wellness programs and trends among midwestern universities. *Journal of the National Intramural-Recreational Sports Association, 11*(2), 28-32.

Pauly, J. T., Palmer, J. A., & Wright, C. C. (1982). The effect of a 14 week employee fitness program on selected physiological and psychological parameters. *Journal of Occupational Medicine, 24,* 457-463.

Reed, R. W., Mulvaney, D. E., & Billingham, R. E. (1986). *Health promotion service evaluation and impact study.* Indianapolis: Benchmarch Press, Inc.

Rudman, W. J., & Steinhardt, M. (1988). Fitness in the workplace: The effects of a corporate health and fitness program on work culture. *Health Values: Achieving High Level Wellness, 12*(2) 4-17.

Seaward, B. S., & Snelling, A. M. (1990). A marketing strategy for a campus wellness program. *Health Education, 21*(5), 4-8.

$$\bar{X} = \frac{\cancel{\sigma}\Sigma X}{N} = \bar{X}$$

$\bar{X}$ $X_1 = \cancel{10}\ 3.3$

$X_2 = 2.5$

Pre-Test 3 Homework

1. What happens to the probability of making a Type I error as we decrease the alpha level from .01 to .05?

2. What happens to to probability of making a Type II error as we decrease the alpha level from .01 to .05?

3. I believe that if I choose a sample at random, I would find that the average weight for men is higher than the average weight for women. State an appropriate Null Hypothesis (H_o).

4. With the data I would collect on question #3, what type of analysis would be appropriate to conduct? *independent T (2 sample T)*

5. Two groups of students, 50 in each group, were matched on grade point average. One group was taught by the lecture method and one groups was taught using interactive video. What type of analysis would be appropriate to conduct? *matched T (dependent T)*

6. When we reject the null hypothesis when it is actually true, what type of error have we made? *Type I*

7. Given: test used: dependent t; alpha level = .05; df = 30; one-tailed test; calculated value = -1.70. What is your decision regarding the null hypothesis? *will see a question like this (look up in table)*
   chart 1.697   *reject the H_o*

8. A professor hypothesizes hat the students who earn C or better spend more time outside of class on the coursework than students who receive D or F. She collects the following data from two samples of students. What does she conclude? (Hint: This is a one-tailed test.) *calculated T value .81 (no significant diff.)*

No of hours per week C or better	D or F	X_1	X_1^2	X_2	X_2^2
8 5	6 3	8	64	6	36
4 3	2 2	4	16	2	4
4 2	1 1	4	16	1	1
2 1	0 5	2	4	0	0
1 3		1	1	3	9
		5	25	2	4
		3	9	1	1
		2	4	5	25
		1	1	20	80
		3	9		
		33	149		

a. H₀: _____
b. H₁: _____
c. Statistical test (be specific): _____
d. Significance level: .05
e. Critical region (one-tailed test): $t_{.05} \geq$ _____
f. Calculated t = (do your calculations below). .81

g. Decision: *no significant difference*

9. A researcher decides to analyze the effects of nutrition on personality. He collects 7 pairs of identical twins and puts one set of pairs on a controlled diet. The other set is allowed to ea whatever he or she wants. A personality inventory is used and the following data are collected. (Hint: This is a two-tailed test.) *matched T – dependent T*

Set 1	Set 2	D	D²
34	32	2	4
44	40	4	16
28	20	8	64
54	36	18	324
55	50	5	25
43	46	-3	9
54	44	10	100
		44	542

a. H₀: *no sign. diff. between pairs of identical twins — nutrition / the control & the other* 6.29
b. H₁: *there is a sign. diff. between the control & the other group*
c. Statistical test (be specific): *dependent T*
d. Significance level: .01
e. Critical region (two-tailed test): $t_{.05} \geq$ 2.447   df = 6 (N-1)
f. Calculated t = (do your calculations below) 2.50

g. Decision: *no significance at .01*

4-24
Chi Square

soap color is an impt. issue
600 people randomly selected (soap buyers)
each get 3 differently pkg.^{same} soap (1-white, 1-red, 1-green)
They are to test to see which they like best

600 cases of soap   red - white - green
probability =   200   200   200   fe - expected number in a category
actually chose =   200   300   100   fo - observed number in a category

How do they actual choices fit with the probabilities.

$$\chi^2 = \sum \frac{(fo - fe)^2}{fe} = \frac{(200-200)^2}{200} + \frac{(300-200)^2}{200} + \frac{(100-200)^2}{200}$$

$$0 \quad + \quad 50 \quad + \quad 50$$

$$\chi^2 = 100$$

add a 10th step — application statement

STATISTICAL INFERENCE: CATEGORICAL VARIABLES

A nonparametric test of significance is one that makes no assumptions concerning the shape of the population distribution and is commonly referred to as a distribution-free test of significance.

The Chi Square test of significance is commonly used with categorical variables.

The one-variable case is often described as the **goodness of fit chi square**. *easy one to do*

The null hypothesis may be tested by the following formula:

$$X^2 = \sum \frac{(fo - fe)^2}{fe}$$

fo — frequency observed
fe — frequency expected

where:

fo = the observed number is a given category

fe = the expected number in that category

The Chi Square **Test of the independence of categorical variables**.

see p. 58

$$X^2 = \sum_{r} \sum_{c} \frac{(fo - fe)^2}{fe}$$

where

$\sum_{r} \sum_{c}$ directs us to sum over both rows and columns

go to Statistics
drag down Cross Tabulations
chose rows + columns
doesn't make any difference which is which
will give you print out like on p. 54

CHI SQUARE HOMEWORK

CHI SQUARE Question 1: There are 20 members in a group. Simple observation leads you to believe that females and males differ in their proportions of eye color. You count eye color by sex and find that 2 males have brown eyes, 8 females have brown eyes, 7 males have blue eyes, and 3 females have blow eyes. Conduct a chi square analysis on the computer, print it out, describe your analysis, and draw conclusions.

SEX	EYE COLOR
female	blue
female	brown
male	brown
male	blue
male	blue
female	brown
male	blue
female	brown
female	brown
female	brown
female	blue
male	blue
male	blue
male	brown
female	blue
male	blue
female	brown
female	brown
male	blue
female	brown

ANSWER THE FOLLOWING:

H0: *There is no significant difference in the proportions of eye color of females & males.*

H1: *There is a significant difference in the proportion of eye color of females & males.*

df: *1*

alpha level: *.02*

table value: *5.412*

calculated X2 value: *5.05*

decision: *We do not reject the H0.*

interpretation: *There is no significant difference in the proportions of eye color of females & males.*

Chi-Square: 5.05   Phi: 0.50
Significance: 0.02   Cramer's V: 0.50

Cell Count Row % Column % Total %	Data File: chi		
	female	male	gender Totals
blue	3 30.00 27.27 15.00	7 70.00 77.78 35.00	10 50.00
brown	8 80.00 72.73 40.00	2 20.00 22.22 10.00	10 50.00
eye color Totals	11 55.00	9 45.00	20 100.00

$$x^2 = \sum_{r}^{r}\sum_{}^{c} \frac{(f_o - f_e)^2}{f_e}$$

where $f_e = \frac{\text{row total}}{\text{grand total}} \times \text{column total}$

#1. $\frac{22}{103} \times 51 = 10.89$

#2. $\frac{22}{103} \times 52 = 11.11$

#3. $\frac{59}{103} \times 51 = 29.2$

#4. $\frac{59}{103} \times 52 = 29.79$

#5. $\frac{22}{103} \times 51 = 10.89$

#6. $\frac{22}{103} \times 52 = 11.11$

#7

The observed was lower

1. A ~~larger~~ smaller proportion of high school graduates said they had higher ~~life~~ satisfaction than expected.

2. A larger proportion of college grads. reported higher life sat. than expected.

3. A larger # of H.S. grads reported lower life satisfaction than expected.

4. A smaller # of college grad. reported a lower life satisfaction than expected.

$\chi^2 = 11.10$

Chi Square Homework question 2. A study was conducted in order to determine if there is a relationship between educational level and life satisfaction. The following data were compiled.

Educational Level

Perceived Life Satisfaction	H.S. Graduate	College Graduate	Total
High	fo 5 / fe 10.89 (3.19)	17 / 11.11 (3.12)	22
Medium	30 / 29.2 (.02)	29 / 29.79 (.021)	59
Low	16 / 10.89 (2.4)	6 / 11.11 (2.35)	22
Totals	51	52	103

calculated X^2 value = 11.10

df = $(r-1)(c-1)$ = 2

alpha level = .05

table value = 5.991

decision = We reject the Ho.

describe the overall picture of these results

make an appropriate application statement — If you want high life satisfaction go to college

$$\frac{(5-10.89)^2}{10.89} + \frac{(17-11.11)^2}{11.11} + \frac{(30-29.2)^2}{29.2} + \frac{(29-29.79)^2}{29.79} + \frac{(16-10.89)^2}{10.89} + \frac{(6-11.11)^2}{11.11} =$$

3.19 + 3.12 + .02 + .021 + 2.4 + 2.35 = 11.101

see back page

1. H_0 = There is no significant difference in the life satisfaction category of high school grads. vs. college grads.

2. H_1 = There is a significant difference in the life satisfaction category of high school grads. vs. college grads.

3. Stat. test = Chi square of independence of categorical variables

4. significance level = .05 alpha level

5. sampling distribution = $df = (r-1)(c-1) = 2$

6. Critical value = 5.991

7. Calculated value = 11.10

8. decision = We reject the H_0.

9. interpretation = There is a difference.

10. Application statement:

Ratios of χ^2

Degrees of freedom df	.10	.05	.02	.01
1	2.706	3.841	5.412	6.635
2	4.605	5.991	7.824	9.210
3	6.251	7.815	9.837	11.341
4	7.779	9.488	11.668	13.277
5	9.236	11.070	13.388	15.086
6	10.645	12.592	15.033	16.812
7	12.017	14.067	16.622	18.475
8	13.362	15.507	18.168	20.090
9	14.684	16.919	19.679	21.666
10	15.987	18.307	21.161	23.209
11	17.275	19.675	22.618	24.725
12	18.549	21.026	24.054	26.217
13	19.812	22.362	25.472	27.688
14	21.064	23.685	26.873	29.141
15	22.307	24.996	28.259	30.578
16	23.542	26.296	29.633	32.000
17	24.769	27.587	30.995	33.409
18	25.989	28.869	32.346	34.805
19	27.204	30.144	33.687	36.191
20	28.412	31.410	35.020	37.566
21	29.615	32.671	36.343	38.932
22	30.813	33.924	37.659	40.289
23	32.007	35.172	38.968	41.638
24	33.196	36.415	40.270	42.980
25	34.382	37.652	41.566	44.314
26	35.563	38.885	42.856	45.642
27	36.741	40.113	44.140	46.963
28	37.916	41.337	45.419	48.278
29	39.087	42.557	46.693	49.588
30	40.256	43.773	47.962	50.892

The 1982 Health Status of the Male Vietnam Veteran

*By C. Alex Waignadt, Ph.D.,
Deborah A. Miller, Ph.D.,
and Lorraine G. Davis, Ph.D.*

There is no doubt that certain physical changes take place in adults as the years pass by. Specific social circumstances may contribute to these changes but the extent of variance is often limited to conjecture. The major concern of this study was to determine if the health status of Vietnam veterans remained consistent with their noncombatant counterparts or if the stress of war (Archibald et al., 1962; Archibald and Tuddenham, 1965) or social reentry (Borus, 1973) significantly influenced health status.

In 1968, Rahe (1968) studied the crews of three United States Navy cruisers, two of which were detached to Vietnam. The study results indicated that the men under most stress developed significantly higher numbers of illnesses. A more recent study conducted by Walker (1981) and sponsored by the Law Enforcement Assistance Administration showed that of the 29,000 men presently incarcerated in state and federal prisons, the vast majority are honorably discharged veterans who have had problems readjusting to civilian life and have developed negative health behaviors such as drug and alcohol abuse problems.

Several studies have attempted to identify the intrapersonal problems associated with involvement in the Vietnam war. None, however, have attempted to predict the long-term outcome with regard to the health status of its participants. Therefore, the thesis of this research centers on the question: What are the long-term physical effects of catastrophic experiences like combat? In particular, what are the effects of the war on the physical health of those who fought it? The hypothesis is: Vietnam veterans will have a lower level of perceived health status than either Vietnam-era veterans or Vietnam-era nonveterans.

METHOD

One hundred and sixty-eight subjects were solicited from agencies, organizations, and schools in West Central Oregon. The Vietnam and Vietnam-era veterans were drawn from an area community college, a veteran's center, and a university veteran's association. The Vietnam-era nonveterans were drawn from the general population of Eugene, Oregon and surrounding communities.

The principal instrument for use in the study was the Cornell Medical Index Health Questionnaire (CMI). The CMI is a self-administered four-page data collection sheet. Two forms, one for men and one for women, exist with only the men's form used. There are 195 questions on the CMI which are chosen to correspond closely to those usually asked in detailed and comprehensive medical interviews. In every case, a "yes" response means that the subject has the symptom(s) about which he is questioned. Technical terms are avoided, but when their use is necessary, an explanation is given. Thus diabetes is explained as "sugar disease," urinate as "passing water," and varicose veins as "swollen veins."

According to Buros (1972) there is no information on the reliability and validity of the CMI. It has, however, been used in many research studies and Buros (1978) indicates that more disease symptoms can be identified through the CMI than through a regular medical review.

In the initial construction of the CMI, items were selected after a pilot study of more than 1,000 subjects had shown that the items collected the data accurately. For research purposes, in this study, the items (195 total) were divided into four categories: (1) those relating to present body symptoms (139 items), (2) those relating to past illnesses (41 items), (3) those related to family history (12 items), and (4) those relating to behavior (3 items). The questions elicit a response to either "yes" or "no" and scoring, for each category, is done by adding the number of "yes" answers. A grand total can be determined by adding the "yes" responses in all four categories. Four scores on the CMI were calculated for each subject and each of the four subtotals served as separate dependent variables.

In addition to the CMI, respondents were asked a question related to the perception of their health status. The response mode was one of three descriptive terms.

RESULTS

Of the 168 men, 48 were Vietnam veterans, 55 were Vietnam-era veterans, and 65 were Vietnam-era nonveterans. The average age of the Vietnam veteran sample was approximately 33 years ($x = 33.33$), while the average age for the Vietnam-era veteran was about 30 ($x = 29.84$), and the Vietnam-era nonveterans averaged approximately 31 years ($x = 30.91$). Due to the slight disparity in age, where this variable was found to be a contributing factor, the groups were matched and a separate analysis was conducted and reported.

Members of each group were asked about their annual doctor visitation rate. Although the three groups were dissimilar with regards to doctor visitation rates (Vietnam veterans averaged 3.28 visitations per year, Vietnam-era veterans averaged 2.19, and Vietnam-era nonveterans averaged 1.60), all three groups were found to be lower than the average for residents of West Central Oregon whose doctor visitation rate per person is 4.5 per year. Age specific data for the population were not available.

In terms of education, income, marital status, occupational level, and religious preference, all three groups were more alike than different. Proportionately, more Vietnam veterans (75%) had dependents than either the Vietnam-era veterans (51%) or the Vietnam-era nonveterans (37%).

The self-reported perceived health status was elicited by the question: "How would you rate your physical health over the last ten years?" Frequency and Chi-square results to this question are presented in Table I.

$$\chi^2 = \sum_{r}^{r}\sum_{}^{c}\frac{(f_o - f_e)^2}{f_e}$$

need cell sizes of at least 5
can collapse cells to create 5

3X3 χ^2 or 3x3 contingency table

	nam	vets	non-vets	total
excellent	(.8) fo 16/20 fe	(.67) 19/22.92	(2.32) 35/27.08	= 70
good	(.02) 20/20.57	(1.25) 29/23.57	(.85) 23/27.86	= 72
fair/poor	(2.81) 12/7.43	(.27) 7/8.51	(.93) 7/10.06	= 26
total	48	55	65	= 168

Chi square for independence of categorical variables

1. H_o = no sign. diff in proportions of categories of veterans for health status
2. H_1 = There is a significant difference in proportions of categories of vets....
3. Stat. test = χ^2 of independence of categorical variables
4. .05 alpha level of significance
5. sampling distrib. = $df = (r-1)(c-1)$ or $(3-1)(3-1) = 4\ df$
6. critical region = 9.488
7. calculated value = $\chi^2 = \sum_{}^{r}\sum_{}^{c}\frac{(f_o - f_e)^2}{f_e}$

χ^2 = where $f_e = \frac{\text{row total}}{\text{grand total}} \times \text{column total}$ (first = figure each one separately)

$$\frac{(16-20)^2}{20} + \frac{(19-22.92)^2}{22.92} + \frac{(35-27.08)^2}{27.08} + \frac{(20-20.57)^2}{20.57} + \frac{(29-23.57)^2}{23.57} +$$

$$\frac{(23-27.86)^2}{27.86} + \frac{(12-7.43)^2}{7.43} + \frac{(7-8.51)^2}{8.51} + \frac{(7-10.06)^2}{10.06} =$$

.8 + .67 + 2.32 + .02 + 1.25 + .85 + 2.81 + .27 + .93

$\chi^2 = 9.92$

8. decision = We reject the H_o.
9. interpretation = (Pick 2-3 cells) There is a larger proportion of nonvets who reported excellent health than we expected. There is also a larger proportion of Nam vets that said they had poor health than we expected.
10. application — Don't go to war if you want to be healthy in later years.

TABLE I. Chi-square Analysis for Physical Health Rating of the Last Ten Years by Military Status

Health Category	Vietnam Vets	Vietnam-era Vets	Vietnam-era Nonvets	Total
Excellent	16	19	35	70
Good	20	29	23	72
Poor	12	7	7	26
Total	48	55	65	168

$x^2 = 9.92*$, df = 4, p < .05

The Chi-square value of 9.92 indicated that there are different proportions of men among the groups reporting the selected health ratings. According to these data, a signficant proportion of Vietnam-era nonveterans reported having "excellent" health while a greater proportion of Vietnam-era veterans had "good" health. Comparatively more Vietnam veterans reported having had less than good health over the last ten years than either of the other two groups studied.

The results of the Cornell Medical Index Health Questionnaire paralleled the self-perceptions in most regards. The results of the mean reponses and statistical comparisons between the study groups in each of the four subcategories are presented in Table II.

TABLE II. Summary of Mean CMI Responses by Military Status

CMI Category		Possible	Vietnam	Veteran Status Vietnam-era	Vietnam-era non	ANOVA F	df	p
Present Illness Symptoms	(a)	139	34.2 (21.7)	11.7 (6.3)	10.1 (9.9)	27.2*	2,82	.05
	(b)	139	27.3 (20.9)	17.0 (14.1)	10.0 (8.1)	18.4*	2,157	.05
Past Illness Symptom		41	5.1 (3.1)	3.9 (1.8)	3.9 (2.6)	3.8*	2,148	.05
Negative Health Behaviors		3	1.5 (.6)	1.2 (.4)	1.3 (.7)	1.6	2,61	n.s.
Family Health History		12	2.1 (1.1)	1.0 (1.5)	1.6 (1.2)	1.0	1.95	n.s.

a) Age-adjusted due to older Vietnam vet group.
b) Not adjusted by age.
Mean
(ST. Dev)

Present Illnesses Symptoms

The scoring range on the instrument category identified as CMI responses related to present illness symptoms are 88 out of a possible 139 points. The overall mean for the entire sample was 17.33. The highest mean score (34.2) was found in the Vietnam veteran group while the lowest mean score (10-1) was located in the Vietnam-era nonveteran group. All three groups had large standard deviations which indicate extensive variability. The Vietnam veterans have the most inconsistency.

The Vietnam veteran's average score indicated that these veterans exhibited approximately 30 percent of the total possible symptoms in the present illness category. By general standards this would be a large number of symptoms to have at any one time. An F ratio of 18.4 indicated that significant differences existed among the three study groups on the present illness symptoms.

Vietnam veterans had more illness symptoms than either Vietnam-era veterans (t = 3.46, df = 97, p = .00) and Vietnam-era nonveterans (t = 6.07, df = 107, p = .00). Additionally, the Vietnam-era veterans had significantly more illness symptoms than the Vietnam-era nonveterans (t = 2.50, df = 111, p = .01) but significantly less symptoms than the Vietnam veterans.

All demographic variables were studies in relation to the present illness symptoms to determine if any were factors in explaining the differences between the groups. Age was the only variable found to be a contributing factor. A separate analysis was conducted with the groups matched on the age variable. In this analysis, the Vietnam veteran group had a mean score on present illness symptoms higher than without age—adjusted but with a similar degree of variability. The Vietnam-era veterans had a lower number of present illness symptoms. The mean scores for the Vietnam-era nonveterans were minimally affected by the age-adjustment. An F ratio of 27.17 indicated the significant differences still remained and, in fact, were more diverse. The Vietnam-era veterans were no longer significantly different than the Vietnam-era nonveterans (t = .41, df = 55, p = .69). These results are consistent with those derived from the self perception "physical health rating over the last ten years" question of the study instrument.

Past Illness Symptoms

The second category for comparison within the CMI involves responses relating to past illness symptoms. The range of scores of CMI responses was found to be 13 out of a possible of 41. The mean was 4.29 overall, so comparatively the Vietnam veterans scored above the grand mean while the other two groups scored below. An F ratio of 3.8 showed that there were significant differences among the three groups on responses to the CMI relating to past illnesses.

Vietnam veterans had more past illness symptoms than either of the other two groups (vets vs era vets, t = 2.43, df = 96, p = .02; vets vs nonvets, t = 2.38, df = 100, p = .02) but Vietnam-era veterans and Vietnam-era nonveterans were not significantly different (t = .09, df = 103, p = .93). The results of these analyses parallel the results found on the "present illness" comparisons.

Negative Health Behaviors

The third category within the CMI involves responses relating to negative health behaviors. These behaviors

were primarily drug-oriented with smoking and drinking practices queried. The possible range for this category was three; however, a large percentage of the individuals in all three groups did not report any negative health behaviors. For those who did report negative health behaviors, an F ratio of 1.6 indicated that the three study groups did not differ on this category.

Since a large proportion of individuals in each group did not report having negative health behaviors, a Chi-square analysis was done with the data reduced to a categorical format. A Chi-square value of 8.31 (df = 2, p v .05) indicated significant differences between groups. A significantly higher proportion of Vietnam veterans practice negative health behaviors than Vietnam-era nonveterans.

TABLE III. Frequency Responses and Chi-Square Results for Negative Health Behaviors by Military Status

Negative Health Behavior Response	Vietnam Vet	Vietnam-era Vet	Vietnam-era Nonvet	Total
Yes	26	20	18	64
No	22	35	47	104
Total	48	55	65	168

$x^2 = 8.31*$, df = 2, $p < .05$

Family Health History

The possible range of scores for the family health history subcategory was 12. A large percentage of individuals did not respond with a "yes" to any of the questions in this category. For those who did indicate a family history of health problems, the three study groups were not different.

Since a large proportion of individuals did not report having family health problems, a Chi-square analysis was done and indicated that the three study groups did not differ ($X^2 = .98$, df = 2, p v .05). Vietnam veterans, Vietnam-era veterans and Vietnam-era nonveterans had similar histories when comparing family health background.

DISCUSSION

The results which require comment are those related to past illness symptoms and negative health behaviors. The interpretation of past illness symptoms is particularly open to different explanations.

For some, past illness symptoms may be interpreted as last week, while for others the past could mean 10 to 15 years ago. There is no way of knowing if these past illness symptoms were pre or postservice occurrences. The symptoms identified may have existed prior to the military or participation in the military may have caused or aggravated them. The Seiling and Page (1980) study indicated that newly discharged servicemen did not suffer from nonveterans in terms of health status. This, coupled with the fact that physically defective persons are rejected from military involvement would lead one to believe that the "past illness symptoms" responded to by the study population are post-service occurrences. Nevertheless, one can only speculate as to whether military involvement caused these symptoms to occur.

One obvious parallel, which can be made, is that of responses on the CMI compared to the responses on the "physical health over the last ten years" question. When comparing the two, results show an overall consistence and the group which subjectively related its health lowest (the Vietnam veteran group), was found to also show low ratings or more symptoms on the CMI.

The relationship between the current presence of illness symptoms and negative health behaviors seems obvious. Participation in health behaviors of a detrimental effect will seemingly reveal themselves in illness symptoms. One of the points worth making is that the present illness symptoms in the CMI are of both a physical and psychological nature. The effects of combat and war activities may have an effect on both types of symptoms. Further studies of the health manifestations seem appropriate. The veterans' treatment centers can expect to have more persons than in the general population needing assistance with illnesses both physical and psychological.

At this point in time the doctor visitation rate between the three study groups did not differ. The relatively poor health status as measured by illness symptoms was not reflected in seeking medical care. As the Vietnam veterans get older and the physical status naturally changes, the need for more medical care will indeed be indicated. This pattern may of course be reversed if the number of negative health behaviors was reduced. This may be accomplished by the assumption of more of the responsibility for health behavior. The Vietnam veteran is especially in need of mechanisms for behavior change and the acquisition of appropriate copying skills.

REFERENCES

Archibald, H., D. Long and C. Miller
1962 "Gross stress reactions in combat: a 15-year follow-up." American Journal of Psychiatry 119: 317-322.

Archibald, H. and R. Tuddenham
1965 "Persistent stress reaction following combat: A 20-year follow-up." Archives of General Psychiatry 12:475-481.

Borus, J.
1973 "Reentry: Adjustment issues facing the Vietnam returnee." Archives of General Psychiatry 28:501-506.

Buros, O.
1972 The Seventh Mental Measurement Yearbook. Cryphon Press, New Jersey.

Buros, O.
1978 The Eighth Mental Measurement Yearbook. Cryphon Press, New Jersey.

ANALYSIS OF VARIANCE (ANOVA)

The acceptable way of comparison multi group means is by using ANOVA. We will do this by looking at the ratio of the variances. There are 2 variances we look at: between group variance and within group variance.

The ratio between these two variances is called the F-ratio and is placed on an F distribution. The larger the between group variance relative to the within group variance, the greater the F ratio and the more significant the differences between the groups.

$$F = \frac{between}{within}$$

The source for the variance both between groups and within groups is their sum of squares.

It is my belief that the quality of life is greater in Missouri than it is in Kansas or Arkansas. I get a panel of experts in quality of life and have them rate the three states.

My null hypothesis would be that there is no difference in quality of life in Missouri, Kansas, or Arkansas as measured by independent experts.

The following data were collected:

Expert	Missouri	Kansas	Arkansas
#1	4	1	3
#2	5	1	2
#3	5	2	3
#4	6	2	4
M	5	1.5	3
sd	.82	.58	.82
Sx	.41	.29	.41

$$Sx = \frac{S}{\sqrt{N-1}}$$

```
       Kan        Ark         Mo
    _____
    1    2     3     4     5     6
```

We are comparing distributions of means. If they are all part of the same distribution, the variances should all be the same.

Within group variance or $SS_w = SS_1 + SS_2 + SS_3$ where: $SS = \sum X^2 - \frac{(\sum X)^2}{N}$

Between group variance or $SS_{bet} = \sum N (M - M_{tot})^2$

It is generally accepted to create a summary table. This table will look something like this:

ANOVA TABLE

VARIANCE	SS	df	MS	F-ratio
Between groups				
Within groups				
Totals				

$df_{bet} = K-1 =$
$df_w = N-K =$

The obtained F-ratio is significant at a given level if it is equal to or greater than the value shown on the table "Critical Values of F."

Critical Values of F

The obtained F is significant at a given level if it is equal to or *greater than* the value shown in the table. 0.05 (light row) and 0.01 (dark row) points for the distribution of F.

df denom	1	2	3	4	5	6	7	8	9	10	11	12	14	16	20	24	30	40	50	75	100	200	500	∞
1	161	200	216	225	230	234	237	239	241	242	243	244	245	246	248	249	250	251	252	253	253	254	254	254
	4052	4999	5403	5625	5764	5859	5928	5981	6022	6056	6082	6106	6142	6169	6208	6234	6258	6286	6302	6323	6334	6352	6361	6366
2	18.51	19.00	19.16	19.25	19.30	19.33	19.36	19.37	19.38	19.39	19.40	19.41	19.42	19.43	19.44	19.45	19.46	19.47	19.47	19.48	19.49	19.49	19.50	19.50
	98.49	99.01	99.17	99.25	99.30	99.33	99.34	99.36	99.38	99.40	99.41	99.42	99.43	99.44	99.45	99.46	99.47	99.48	99.48	99.49	99.49	99.49	99.50	99.50
3	10.13	9.55	9.28	9.12	9.01	8.94	8.88	8.84	8.81	8.78	8.76	8.74	8.71	8.69	8.66	8.64	8.62	8.60	8.58	8.57	8.56	8.54	8.54	8.53
	34.12	30.81	29.46	28.71	28.24	27.91	27.67	27.49	27.34	27.23	27.13	27.05	26.92	26.83	26.69	26.60	26.50	26.41	26.30	26.27	26.23	26.18	26.14	26.12
4	7.71	6.94	6.59	6.39	6.26	6.16	6.09	6.04	6.00	5.96	5.93	5.91	5.87	5.84	5.80	5.77	5.74	5.71	5.70	5.68	5.66	5.65	5.64	5.63
	21.20	18.00	16.69	15.98	15.52	15.21	14.98	14.80	14.66	14.54	14.45	14.37	14.24	14.15	14.02	13.93	13.83	13.74	13.69	13.61	13.57	13.52	13.48	13.46
5	6.61	5.79	5.41	5.19	5.05	4.95	4.88	4.82	4.78	4.74	4.70	4.68	4.64	4.60	4.56	4.53	4.50	4.46	4.44	4.42	4.40	4.38	4.37	4.36
	16.26	13.27	12.06	11.39	10.97	10.67	10.45	10.27	10.15	10.05	9.96	9.89	9.77	9.68	9.55	9.47	9.38	9.29	9.24	9.17	9.13	9.07	9.04	9.02
6	5.99	5.14	4.76	4.53	4.39	4.28	4.21	4.15	4.10	4.06	4.03	4.00	3.96	3.92	3.87	3.84	3.81	3.77	3.75	3.72	3.71	3.69	3.68	3.67
	13.74	10.92	9.78	9.15	8.75	8.47	8.26	8.10	7.98	7.87	7.79	7.72	7.60	7.52	7.39	7.31	7.23	7.14	7.09	7.02	6.99	6.94	6.90	6.88
7	5.59	4.74	4.35	4.12	3.97	3.87	3.79	3.73	3.68	3.63	3.60	3.57	3.52	3.49	3.44	3.41	3.38	3.34	3.32	3.29	3.28	3.25	3.24	3.23
	12.25	9.55	8.45	7.85	7.46	7.19	7.00	6.84	6.71	6.62	6.54	6.47	6.35	6.27	6.15	6.07	5.98	5.90	5.85	5.78	5.75	5.70	5.67	5.65
8	5.32	4.46	4.07	3.84	3.69	3.58	3.50	3.44	3.39	3.34	3.31	3.28	3.23	3.20	3.15	3.12	3.08	3.05	3.03	3.00	2.98	2.96	2.94	2.93
	11.26	8.65	7.59	7.01	6.63	6.37	6.19	6.03	5.91	5.82	5.74	5.67	5.56	5.48	5.36	5.28	5.20	5.11	5.06	5.00	4.96	4.91	4.88	4.86
9	5.12	4.26	3.86	3.63	3.48	3.37	3.29	3.23	3.18	3.13	3.10	3.07	3.02	2.98	2.93	2.90	2.86	2.82	2.80	2.77	2.76	2.73	2.72	2.71
	10.56	8.02	6.99	6.42	6.06	5.80	5.62	5.47	5.35	5.26	5.18	5.11	5.00	4.92	4.80	4.73	4.64	4.56	4.51	4.45	4.41	4.36	4.33	4.31
10	4.96	4.10	3.71	3.48	3.33	3.22	3.14	3.07	3.02	2.97	2.94	2.91	2.86	2.82	2.77	2.74	2.70	2.67	2.64	2.61	2.59	2.56	2.55	2.54
	10.04	7.56	6.55	5.99	5.64	5.39	5.21	5.06	4.95	4.85	4.78	4.71	4.60	4.52	4.41	4.33	4.25	4.17	4.12	4.05	4.01	3.96	3.93	3.91
11	4.84	3.98	3.59	3.36	3.20	3.09	3.01	2.95	2.90	2.86	2.82	2.79	2.74	2.70	2.65	2.61	2.57	2.53	2.50	2.47	2.45	2.42	2.41	2.40
	9.65	7.20	6.22	5.67	5.32	5.07	4.88	4.74	4.63	4.54	4.46	4.40	4.29	4.21	4.10	4.02	3.94	3.86	3.80	3.74	3.70	3.66	3.62	3.60
12	4.75	3.88	3.49	3.26	3.11	3.00	2.92	2.85	2.80	2.76	2.72	2.69	2.64	2.60	2.54	2.50	2.46	2.42	2.40	2.36	2.35	2.32	2.31	2.30
	9.33	6.93	5.95	5.41	5.06	4.82	4.65	4.50	4.39	4.30	4.22	4.16	4.05	3.98	3.86	3.78	3.70	3.61	3.56	3.49	3.46	3.41	3.38	3.36
13	4.67	3.80	3.41	3.18	3.02	2.92	2.84	2.77	2.72	2.67	2.63	2.60	2.55	2.51	2.46	2.42	2.38	2.34	2.32	2.28	2.26	2.24	2.22	2.21
	9.07	6.70	5.74	5.20	4.86	4.62	4.44	4.30	4.19	4.10	4.02	3.96	3.85	3.78	3.67	3.59	3.51	3.42	3.37	3.30	3.27	3.21	3.18	3.16
14	4.60	3.74	3.34	3.11	2.96	2.85	2.77	2.70	2.65	2.60	2.56	2.53	2.48	2.44	2.39	2.35	2.31	2.27	2.24	2.21	2.19	2.16	2.14	2.13
	8.86	6.51	5.56	5.03	4.69	4.46	4.28	4.14	4.03	3.94	3.86	3.80	3.70	3.62	3.51	3.43	3.34	3.26	3.21	3.14	3.11	3.06	3.02	3.00
15	4.54	3.68	3.29	3.06	2.90	2.79	2.70	2.64	2.59	2.55	2.51	2.48	2.43	2.39	2.33	2.29	2.25	2.21	2.18	2.15	2.12	2.10	2.08	2.07
	8.68	6.36	5.42	4.89	4.56	4.32	4.14	4.00	3.89	3.80	3.73	3.67	3.56	3.48	3.36	3.29	3.20	3.12	3.07	3.00	2.97	2.92	2.89	2.87
16	4.49	3.63	3.24	3.01	2.85	2.74	2.66	2.59	2.54	2.49	2.45	2.42	2.37	2.33	2.28	2.24	2.20	2.16	2.13	2.09	2.07	2.04	2.02	2.01
	8.53	6.23	5.29	4.77	4.44	4.20	4.03	3.89	3.78	3.69	3.61	3.55	3.45	3.37	3.25	3.18	3.10	3.01	2.96	2.89	2.86	2.80	2.77	2.75
17	4.45	3.59	3.20	2.96	2.81	2.70	2.62	2.55	2.50	2.45	2.41	2.38	2.33	2.29	2.23	2.19	2.15	2.11	2.08	2.04	2.02	1.99	1.97	1.96
	8.40	6.11	5.18	4.67	4.34	4.10	3.93	3.79	3.68	3.59	3.52	3.45	3.35	3.27	3.16	3.08	3.00	2.92	2.86	2.79	2.76	2.70	2.67	2.65
18	4.41	3.55	3.16	2.93	2.77	2.66	2.58	2.51	2.46	2.41	2.37	2.34	2.29	2.25	2.19	2.15	2.11	2.07	2.04	2.00	1.98	1.95	1.93	1.92
	8.28	6.01	5.09	4.58	4.25	4.01	3.85	3.71	3.60	3.51	3.44	3.37	3.27	3.19	3.07	3.00	2.91	2.83	2.78	2.71	2.68	2.62	2.59	2.57
19	4.38	3.52	3.13	2.90	2.74	2.63	2.55	2.48	2.43	2.38	2.34	2.31	2.26	2.21	2.15	2.11	2.07	2.02	2.00	1.96	1.94	1.91	1.90	1.88
	8.18	5.93	5.01	4.50	4.17	3.94	3.77	3.63	3.52	3.43	3.36	3.30	3.19	3.12	3.00	2.92	2.84	2.76	2.70	2.63	2.60	2.54	2.51	2.49
20	4.35	3.49	3.10	2.87	2.71	2.60	2.52	2.45	2.40	2.35	2.31	2.28	2.23	2.18	2.12	2.08	2.04	1.99	1.96	1.92	1.90	1.87	1.85	1.84
	8.10	5.85	4.94	4.43	4.10	3.87	3.71	3.56	3.45	3.37	3.30	3.23	3.13	3.05	2.94	2.86	2.77	2.69	2.63	2.56	2.53	2.47	2.44	2.42
21	4.32	3.47	3.07	2.84	2.68	2.57	2.49	2.42	2.37	2.32	2.28	2.25	2.20	2.15	2.09	2.05	2.00	1.96	1.93	1.80	1.87	1.84	1.82	1.81
	8.02	5.78	4.87	4.37	4.04	3.81	3.65	3.51	3.40	3.31	3.24	3.17	3.07	2.99	2.88	2.80	2.72	2.63	2.58	2.51	2.47	2.42	2.38	2.36
22	4.30	3.44	3.05	2.82	2.66	2.55	2.47	2.40	2.35	2.30	2.26	2.23	2.18	2.13	2.07	2.03	1.98	1.93	1.91	1.87	1.84	1.81	1.80	1.78
	7.94	5.72	4.82	4.31	3.99	3.76	3.59	3.45	3.35	3.26	3.18	3.12	3.02	2.94	2.83	2.75	2.67	2.58	2.53	2.46	2.42	2.37	2.33	2.31
23	4.28	3.42	3.03	2.80	2.64	2.53	2.45	2.38	2.32	2.28	2.24	2.20	2.14	2.10	2.04	2.00	1.96	1.91	1.88	1.84	1.82	1.79	1.77	1.76
	7.88	5.66	4.76	4.26	3.94	3.71	3.54	3.41	3.30	3.21	3.14	3.07	2.97	2.89	2.78	2.70	2.62	2.53	2.48	2.41	2.37	2.32	2.28	2.26
24	4.26	3.40	3.01	2.78	2.62	2.51	2.43	2.36	2.30	2.26	2.22	2.18	2.13	2.09	2.02	1.98	1.94	1.89	1.86	1.82	1.80	1.76	1.74	1.73
	7.82	5.61	4.72	4.22	3.90	3.67	3.50	3.36	3.25	3.17	3.09	3.03	2.93	2.85	2.74	2.66	2.58	2.49	2.44	2.36	2.33	2.27	2.23	2.21
25	4.24	3.38	2.99	2.76	2.60	2.49	2.41	2.34	2.28	2.24	2.20	2.16	2.11	2.06	2.00	1.96	1.92	1.87	1.84	1.80	1.77	1.74	1.72	1.71
	7.77	5.57	4.68	4.18	3.86	3.63	3.46	3.32	3.21	3.13	3.05	2.99	2.89	2.81	2.70	2.62	2.54	2.45	2.40	2.32	2.29	2.23	2.19	2.17
26	4.22	3.37	2.89	2.74	2.59	2.47	2.39	2.32	2.27	2.22	2.18	2.15	2.10	2.05	1.99	1.95	1.90	1.85	1.82	1.78	1.76	1.72	1.70	1.69
	7.72	5.53	4.64	4.14	3.82	3.59	3.42	3.29	3.17	3.09	3.02	2.96	2.86	2.77	2.66	2.58	2.50	2.41	2.36	2.28	2.25	2.19	2.15	2.13
27	4.21	3.35	2.96	2.73	2.57	2.46	2.37	2.30	2.25	2.20	2.16	2.13	2.08	2.03	1.97	1.93	1.88	1.84	1.80	1.76	1.74	1.71	1.68	1.67
	7.68	5.49	4.60	4.11	3.79	3.56	3.39	3.26	3.14	3.06	2.98	2.93	2.83	2.74	2.63	2.55	2.47	2.38	2.33	2.25	2.21	2.16	2.12	2.10
28	4.20	3.34	2.95	2.71	2.56	2.44	2.36	2.29	3.24	2.19	2.15	2.12	2.06	2.02	1.96	1.91	1.87	1.81	1.78	1.75	1.72	1.69	1.67	1.65
	7.64	5.45	4.57	4.07	3.76	3.53	3.36	3.23	3.11	3.03	2.95	2.90	2.80	2.71	2.60	2.52	2.44	2.35	2.30	2.22	2.18	2.13	2.09	2.06
29	4.18	3.33	2.93	2.70	2.54	2.43	2.35	2.28	2.22	2.18	2.14	2.10	2.05	2.00	1.94	1.90	1.85	1.80	1.77	1.73	1.71	1.68	1.65	1.64
	7.60	5.52	4.54	4.04	3.73	3.50	3.33	3.20	3.08	3.00	2.92	2.87	2.77	2.68	2.57	2.49	2.41	2.32	2.27	2.19	2.15	2.10	2.06	2.03
30	4.17	3.32	2.92	2.69	2.53	2.42	2.34	2.27	2.21	2.16	2.12	2.09	2.04	1.99	1.93	1.89	1.84	1.79	1.76	1.72	1.69	1.66	1.64	1.62
	7.56	5.39	4.51	4.02	3.70	3.47	3.30	3.17	3.06	2.98	2.90	2.84	2.74	2.66	2.55	2.47	2.38	2.29	2.24	2.16	2.13	2.07	2.03	2.01
32	4.15	3.30	2.90	2.67	2.51	2.40	2.32	2.25	2.19	2.14	2.10	2.07	2.02	1.97	1.91	1.86	1.82	1.76	1.74	1.69	1.67	1.64	1.61	1.59
	7.50	5.34	4.46	3.97	3.66	3.42	3.25	3.12	3.01	2.94	2.86	2.80	2.70	2.62	2.51	2.42	2.34	2.25	2.20	2.12	2.08	2.02	1.98	1.96
34	4.13	3.28	2.88	2.65	2.49	2.38	2.30	2.23	2.17	2.12	2.08	2.05	2.00	1.95	1.89	1.84	1.80	1.74	1.71	1.67	1.64	1.61	1.59	1.57
	7.44	5.29	4.42	3.93	3.61	3.38	3.21	3.08	2.97	2.89	2.82	2.76	2.66	2.58	2.47	2.38	2.30	2.21	2.15	2.08	2.04	1.98	1.94	1.91

		Degrees of freedom for numerator																						
		1	2	3	4	5	6	7	8	9	10	11	12	14	16	20	24	30	40	50	75	100	200	500	∞
Degrees of freedom for denominator	36	4.11 / 7.39	3.26 / 5.25	2.86 / 4.38	2.63 / 3.89	2.48 / 3.58	2.36 / 3.35	2.28 / 3.18	2.21 / 3.04	2.15 / 2.94	2.10 / 2.86	2.06 / 2.78	2.03 / 2.72	1.89 / 2.62	1.93 / 2.54	1.87 / 2.43	1.82 / 2.35	1.78 / 2.26	1.72 / 2.17	1.69 / 2.12	1.65 / 2.04	1.62 / 2.00	1.59 / 1.94	1.56 / 1.90	1.55 / 1.87
	38	4.10 / 7.35	3.25 / 5.21	2.85 / 4.34	2.62 / 3.86	2.46 / 3.54	2.35 / 3.32	2.26 / 3.15	2.19 / 3.02	2.14 / 2.91	2.09 / 2:82	2.05 / 2.75	2.02 / 2.69	1.96 / 2.59	1.92 / 2.51	1.85 / 2.40	1.80 / 2.32	1.76 / 2.22	1.71 / 2.14	1.67 / 2.08	1.63 / 2.00	1.60 / 1.97	1.57 / 1.90	1.54 / 1.86	1.53 / 1.84
	40	4.08 / 7.31	3.23 / 5.18	2.84 / 4.31	2.61 / 3.83	2.45 / 3.51	2.34 / 3.29	2.25 / 3.12	2.18 / 2.99	2.12 / 2.88	2.07 / 2.80	2.04 / 2.73	2.00 / 2.66	1.95 / 2.56	1.90 / 2.49	1.84 / 2.37	1.79 / 2.29	1.74 / 2.20	1.69 / 2.11	1.66 / 2.05	1.61 / 1.97	1.59 / 1.94	1.55 / 1.88	1.53 / 1.84	1.51 / 1.81
	42	4.07 / 7.27	3.22 / 5.15	2.83 / 4.29	2.59 / 3.80	2.44 / 3.49	2.32 / 3.26	2.24 / 3.10	2.17 / 2.96	2.11 / 2.86	2.06 / 2.77	2.02 / 2.70	1.99 / 2.64	1.94 / 2.54	1.89 / 2.46	1.82 / 2.35	1.78 / 2.26	1.73 / 2.17	1.68 / 2.08	1.64 / 2.02	1.60 / 1.94	1.57 / 1.91	1.54 / 1.85	1.51 / 1.80	1.49 / 1.78
	44	4.06 / 7.24	3.21 / 5.12	2.82 / 4.26	2.58 / 3.78	2.43 / 3.46	2.31 / 3.24	2.23 / 3.07	2.16 / 2.94	2.10 / 2.84	2.05 / 2.75	2.01 / 2.68	1.98 / 2.62	1.92 / 2.52	1.88 / 2.44	1.81 / 2.32	1.76 / 2.24	1.72 / 2.15	1.66 / 2.06	1.63 / 2.09	1.58 / 1.92	1.56 / 1.88	1.52 / 1.82	1.50 / 1.78	1.48 / 1.75
	46	4.05 / 7.21	3.20 / 5.10	2.81 / 4.24	2.57 / 3.76	2.42 / 3.44	2.30 / 3.22	2.22 / 3.05	2.14 / 2.92	2.09 / 2.82	2.04 / 2.73	2.00 / 2.66	1.97 / 2.60	1.91 / 2.50	1.87 / 2.42	1.80 / 2.30	1.75 / 2.22	1.71 / 2.13	1.65 / 2.04	1.62 / 1.98	1.57 / 1.90	1.54 / 1.86	1.51 / 1.80	1.48 / 1.76	1.46 / 1.72
	48	4.04 / 7.19	3.19 / 5.08	2.80 / 4.22	2.56 / 3.74	2.41 / 3.42	2.30 / 3.20	2.21 / 3.04	2.14 / 2.90	2.08 / 2.80	2.03 / 2.71	1.99 / 2.64	1.96 / 2.58	1.90 / 2.48	1.86 / 2.40	1.79 / 2.28	1.74 / 2.20	1.70 / 2.11	1.64 / 2.02	1.61 / 1.96	1.56 / 1.88	1.53 / 1.84	1.50 / 1.78	1.47 / 1.73	1.45 / 1.70
	50	4.03 / 7.17	3.18 / 5.06	2.79 / 4.20	2.56 / 3.72	2.40 / 3.41	2.29 / 3.18	2.20 / 3.02	2.13 / 2.88	2.07 / 2.78	2.02 / 2.70	1.98 / 2.62	1.95 / 2.56	1.90 / 2.46	1.85 / 2.39	1.78 / 2.26	1.74 / 2.18	1.69 / 2.10	1.63 / 2.00	1.60 / 1.94	1.55 / 1.86	1.52 / 1.82	1.48 / 1.76	1.46 / 1.71	1.44 / 1.68
	55	4.02 / 7.12	3.17 / 5.01	2.78 / 4.16	2.54 / 3.68	2.38 / 3.37	2.27 / 3.15	2.18 / 2.98	2.11 / 2.85	2.05 / 2.75	2.00 / 2.66	1.97 / 2.59	1.93 / 2.53	1.88 / 2.43	1.83 / 2.35	1.76 / 2.23	1.72 / 2.15	1.67 / 2.06	1.61 / 1.96	1.58 / 1.90	1.52 / 1.82	1.50 / 1.78	1.46 / 1.71	1.43 / 1.66	1.41 / 1.64
	60	4.00 / 7.08	3.15 / 4.98	2.76 / 4.13	2.52 / 3.65	2.37 / 3.34	2.25 / 3.12	2.17 / 2.95	2.10 / 2.82	2.04 / 2.72	1.99 / 2.63	1.95 / 2.56	1.92 / 2.50	1.86 / 2.40	1.81 / 2.32	1.75 / 2.20	1.70 / 2.12	1.65 / 2.03	1.59 / 1.93	1.56 / 1.87	1.50 / 1.79	1.48 / 1.74	1.44 / 1.68	1.41 / 1.63	1.39 / 1.60
	65	3.99 / 7.04	3.14 / 4.95	2.75 / 4.10	2.51 / 3.62	2.36 / 3.31	2.24 / 3.09	2.15 / 2.93	2.08 / 2.79	2.02 / 2.70	1.98 / 2.61	1.94 / 2.54	1.90 / 2.47	1.85 / 2.37	1.80 / 2.30	1.73 / 2.18	1.68 / 2.09	1.63 / 2.00	1.57 / 1.90	1.54 / 1.84	1.49 / 1.76	1.46 / 1.71	1.42 / 1.64	1.39 / 1.60	1.37 / 1.56
	70	3.98 / 7.01	3.13 / 4.92	2.74 / 4.08	2.50 / 3.60	2.35 / 3.29	2.32 / 3.07	2.14 / 2.91	2.07 / 2.77	2.01 / 2.67	1.97 / 2.59	1.93 / 2.51	1.89 / 2.45	1.84 / 2.35	1.79 / 2.28	1.72 / 2.15	1.67 / 2.07	1.62 / 1.98	1.56 / 1.88	1.53 / 1.82	1.47 / 1.74	1.45 / 1.69	1.40 / 1.62	1.37 / 1.56	1.35 / 1.53
	80	3.96 / 6.96	3.11 / 4.88	2.72 / 4.04	2.48 / 3.56	2.33 / 3.25	2.21 / 3.04	2.12 / 2.87	2.05 / 2.74	1.99 / 2.64	1.95 / 2.55	1.91 / 2.48	1.88 / 2.41	1.82 / 2.32	1.77 / 2.24	1.70 / 2.11	1.65 / 2.03	1.60 / 1.94	1.54 / 1.84	1.51 / 1.78	1.45 / 1.70	1.42 / 1.65	1.38 / 1.57	1.35 / 1.52	1.32 / 1.49
	100	3.94 / 6.90	3.09 / 4.82	2.70 / 3.98	2.46 / 3.51	2.30 / 3.20	2.19 / 2.99	2.10 / 2.82	2.03 / 2.69	1.97 / 2.59	1.92 / 2.51	1.88 / 2.43	1.85 / 2.36	1.79 / 2.26	1.75 / 2.19	1.68 / 2.06	1.63 / 1.98	1.57 / 1.89	1.51 / 1.79	1.48 / 1.73	1.42 / 1.64	1.39 / 1.59	1.34 / 1.51	1.30 / 1.46	1.28 / 1.43
	125	3.92 / 6.84	3.07 / 4.78	2.68 / 3.94	2.44 / 3.47	2.29 / 3.17	2.17 / 2.95	2.08 / 2.79	2.01 / 2.65	1.95 / 2.56	1.90 / 2.47	1.86 / 2.40	1.83 / 2.33	1.77 / 2.23	1.72 / 2.15	1.65 / 2.03	1.60 / 1.94	1.55 / 1.85	1.49 / 1.75	1.45 / 1.68	1.39 / 1.59	1.36 / 1.54	1.31 / 1.46	1.27 / 1.40	1.25 / 1.37
	150	3.91 / 6.81	3.06 / 4.75	2.67 / 3.91	2.43 / 3.44	2.27 / 3.13	2.16 / 2.92	2.07 / 2.76	2.00 / 2.62	1.94 / 2.53	1.89 / 2.44	1.85 / 2.37	1.82 / 2.30	1.76 / 2.20	1.71 / 2.12	1.64 / 2.00	1.59 / 1.91	1.54 / 1.83	1.47 / 1.72	1.44 / 1.66	1.37 / 1.56	1.34 / 1.51	1.29 / 1.43	1.25 / 1.37	1.22 / 1.33
	200	3.89 / 6.76	3.04 / 4.71	2.65 / 3.38	2.41 / 3.41	2.26 / 3.11	2.14 / 2.90	2.05 / 2.73	1.98 / 2.60	1.92 / 2.50	1.87 / 2.41	1.83 / 2.34	1.80 / 2.28	1.74 / 1.17	1.69 / 2.09	1.62 / 1.97	1.57 / 1.88	1.52 / 1.79	1.45 / 1.69	1.42 / 1.62	1.35 / 1.53	1.32 / 1.48	1.26 / 1.39	1.22 / 1.33	1.19 / 1.28
	400	3.86 / 6.70	3.02 / 4.66	2.62 / 3.83	2.39 / 3.36	2.23 / 3.06	2.12 / 2.85	2.03 / 2.69	1.96 / 2.55	1.90 / 2.46	1.85 / 2.37	1.81 / 2.29	1.78 / 2.23	1.72 / 2.12	1.67 / 2.04	1.60 / 1.92	1.54 / 1.84	1.49 / 1.74	1.42 / 1.64	1.38 / 1.57	1.32 / 1.47	1.28 / 1.42	1.22 / 1.32	1.16 / 1.24	1.13 / 1.19
	1000	3.85 / 6.66	3.00 / 4.62	2.61 / 3.80	2.38 / 3.34	2.22 / 3.04	2.10 / 2.82	2.02 / 2.66	1.95 / 2.53	1.89 / 2.43	1.84 / 2.34	1.80 / 2.26	1.76 / 2.20	1.70 / 2.09	1.65 / 2.01	1.58 / 1.89	1.53 / 1.81	1.47 / 1.71	1.41 / 1.61	1.36 / 1.54	1.30 / 1.44	1.26 / 1.38	1.19 / 1.28	1.13 / 1.19	1.08 / 1.11
	∞	3.84 / 6.64	2.99 / 4.60	2.60 / 3.78	2.37 / 3.32	2.21 / 3.02	2.09 / 2.80	2.01 / 2.64	1.94 / 2.51	1.88 / 2.41	1.83 / 2.32	1.79 / 2.24	1.75 / 2.18	1.69 / 2.07	1.64 / 1.99	1.57 / 1.87	1.52 / 1.79	1.46 / 1.69	1.40 / 1.59	1.35 / 1.52	1.28 / 1.41	1.24 / 1.36	1.17 / 1.25	1.11 / 1.15	1.00 / 1.00

Project Info.

1. Quest. 1 — means, S.D. and other stuff on program
   descriptive stats on all data (interval data)

2. go thru each question 1-9 & show print-outs

nominal data for both — 2. Blue eyes & others
Blonde hair & others

(one case T)
column with all women
direct program to compare

R 370 Project

Directions: This project is not a team effort, each class member should do his or her own work. Make sure to include your computer printouts in order to get full credit. Question 1 asks you to descriptively profile our class. Questions 2 to 6 will require you to choose the most appropriate analytic technique, conduct the analysis, and answer the question. Use an alpha level of .05 to make your decision. *(Won't accept anything in handwriting)*

1. Describe the demographic data collected on our class in terms of means, standard deviations, etc. *(print-out) (interval data only) Make statements from print-outs.*

2. Are blue eyed people more likely to have blond hair than people with other color eyes? χ^2 *analysis (cross tabulation) print outs*

3. Is the correlation between age and intimidation positive and high? If not, what is it? *show print-out + Pearson R (Regression menu) simple regression coefficient of correlation*

4. Do the males in our class weight more than the females? *Yes. Males-Females Independent t-test — 2 columns of #'s Males Females (unpaired t)* *(probably do manually, enter #'s manually)*

5. Given: The mean height of women in our country is 64 inches. Are the women in our class significantly taller than the population average? *Calculate mean score for women in this class (one case t) 2 columns 1 of #'s — other 64"*

6. Do undergraduate students take more credit hours than graduate students? *independent t (same as #4.)*

Comparing Pharmacology Instruction

Comparative Analysis of Pharmacology Curricula in Schools of Dentistry, Medicine and Optometry

Alex Waigandt*
Edward H. Montgomery**
Glenn T. Housholder***
Marti G. Waigandt****
Dale W. Evans*****

During the past decade a plethora of new drugs have been developed and marketed. Some of these pharmacologic agents, such as long-acting local anesthetics, newer antibacterial, antifungal and antiviral agents, newer agents useful in conscious sedation regiments, newer non-steroidal anti-inflammatory drugs, and agents used in the prevention of oral disease, have direct application to the general practice of dentistry. Current emphasis on cardiovascular diseases has resulted in the development of a myriad of new agents in addition to the continued use of mainstay agents such as digitalis and diuretics. The phenomenal advances in medicine, leading to increased life span, and the emphasis on preventive dentistry has mandated continuing dental care in geriatric patients and thus, necessitates an additional area of applied therapeutics, geriatric pharmacology. Furthermore, patients today demand that dental treatment be efficient, cost-effective, anxiety-free, and painless. This can be partially accomplished through the use of conscious sedation techniques which, because of the availability of newer opioid and benzodiazepine derivatives with increased efficacy and safety,[1] may be feasible for general practitioners. While all of this training can be provided, it requires additional time in the dental curriculum so that the adequacy of training in basic pharmacological principles and traditional therapeutics will not be compromised. As one might suspect, additions to the already overcrowded, continuously escalating undergraduate dental curriculum would not be well accepted by dental administrators. In fact, there is an increasing concept that the basic sciences in the undergraduate dental curriculum are too extensive.[2] Although pharmacology as a discipline is an applied clinical science as well as a basic science, it is not invulnerable to such attacks. In contrast, there is a consensus among some students surveyed that their pharmacology training is inadequate.[3]

There is one previous publication which investigated the teaching of pharmacology in dental schools as compared to other professional schools. Aviado (1972) analyzed data from dental schools, pharmacy schools, and medical schools. However, this survey did not report the number of didactic hours spent on each of the major areas of pharmacology, since the data was expressed as of total hours, which varied widely.[4] Pharmacology percentages training in 58 dental schools in the United States and Canada was examined in 1976, although this study did not make any comparisons with other professional schools involved with teaching drug therapy.[5]

Curricular Guidelines in Pharmacology were developed by the Section on Pharmacology and Therapeutics, American Association of Dental Schools, and published in 1982.[6] While these are recommendations only, the guidelines should be useful in defining areas of study for the dental pharmacology curriculum. Information regarding the use of these guidelines or current teaching trends in pharmacology and therapeutics in U.S. dental schools has not been published. Since the licensed dentist can utilize or prescribe any drugs relevant to the management of oral health problems, it is of interest to determine the current status of pharmacology training in U.S. dental schools as compared to schools of medicine and optometry. Therefore, the objective this survey was to obtain inform

---

*Alex Waigandt, Ph.D., Assistant Professor, Department of HPER, University of Houston.

**Edward H. Montgomery, Ph.D., Professor, Department of Pharmacology, University of Texas at Houston.

***Glenn T. Housholder, Ph.D., Professor, Department of Pharmacology, University of Texas at Houston.

****Marti G. Waigandt, B.S., Student, School of Optometry, University of Houston.

*****Dale W. Evans, H.S.D., Associate Professor, Department of HPER, University of Houston.

tion regarding the status of training in pharmacology for the dental student in reference to students in other health professions.

Methods

The 14 states which contain colleges of dentistry, medicine, and optometry were designated as study states. The states were Alabama, California, Illinois, Indiana, Massachusetts, Michigan, Missouri, New York, Ohio, Oklahoma, Oregon, Pennsylvania, Tennessee, and Texas. Thirty-one colleges of dentistry, 37 colleges of medicine, and 15 schools of optometry received the survey instrument (which is available upon request). The department chairperson or director of pharmacology in each school was identified as the study respondent.

Data were generated from the subjects' responses to the instrument whose purpose was to query the amount of hours devoted to the study of pharmacology. The instrument was designed to reflect the table of contents of a major textbook[7] used in pharmacology courses in dental schools[5] and other professional schools.

The investigation, being descriptive in nature,[8] viewed hours spent in each of 13 major areas of pharmacology as separate dependent variables. These categories included: (1) basic principles in pharmacology, (2) drug effects on the nervous system, (3) psychopharmacology, (4) central nervous system depressants and stimulants, (5) anesthetics, (6) cardiovascular agents, (7) ocular pharmacology, (8) respiratory and gastrointestinal tract agents, (9) endocrine pharmacology, (10) chemotherapy, (11) poisons and antidotes, (12) drug interactions, and (13) prescription writing. A fourteenth variable involved the total hours each school type spends on the study of pharmacology. The categories purposefully were kept broad in order to be indicative of a pharmacology education in various health care professional schools whose educational goals differ. However, each broad category was clearly defined in the survey instrument regarding content. For example, category IV, Central Nervous System Depressants and Stimulants, was identified by the following drug groups: hypnotics, CNS stimulants of the convulsant type, anti-epileptic drugs, narcotic analgesics, and anti-inflammatory drugs.

Results from the instrument were analyzed using the statistical package for the social sciences (SPSS) and calculated on an AS 9000 computer. Treatment of the data was performed implementing: descriptive tables utilized to analyze (1) means, standard deviations, and analysis of variance (ANOVA) to analyze the major study categories; and (2) comparative analyses on the major study categories whose F-ratio indicated significant differences. The .050 level was selected for statistical significance.

Results

Of the 83 schools surveyed, 46 schools responded (55.4% response rate overall). Fifteen were schools of dentistry (48.4% response rate), 20 were schools of medicine (54.0% response rate), and 11 were schools of optometry (73.3% response rate). The results of the study questionnaire are presented in Tables 1 and 2. Table 1 presents means, standard deviations, total range of hours, and analysis of variance of classroom hours spent on major areas of pharmacology (categories) in the different types of institutions.

Table 2 compares those categories, where F-ratios indicate significant differences, between the different types of schools.

Discussion

This survey presents some revealing quantitative information concerning the teaching of pharmacology in three types of professional schools whose educational goals and clinical skills are unique to each profession. In selected areas, which are not related to the major educational goal of the profession, there is great similarity in teaching hours. For example, in prescription writing, drug interactions, respiratory and GI tract medications, endocrine drugs, psychopharmacology, and CNS depressants and stimulants, there are no significant differences in time devoted to these subjects. All three types of professional schools share the importance of instruction in specific areas of pharmacology: basic principles, cardiovascular agents, drugs affecting the nervous system, and chemotherapeutic agents. Although the lecture hours differ significantly between the medical schools and each of the other schools, these areas of instruction constitute a major proportion of each of the curricula. It is noteworthy that the average hours in the dental curriculum utilized in teaching basic principles reported in this study is apparently less than those stated in 1976 ($\bar{X}=6.87$ vs $\bar{X}=10.7$).[5]

There are significant differences in teaching pharmacology in areas of major concern to the individual professions. Schools of optometry averaged 29 hours of lecture in

Table 1. Means, Standard Deviations and Analysis of Variance of Class Lecture Hours Spent on Major Pharmacological Study Categories by Dental, Medical and Optometry Schools

Category	Dental N=15 X̄ (SD)	Medical N=20 X̄ (SD)	Optometry N=11 X̄ (SD)	Grand Mean (SD)	Total Range of Hours	F—ratio	F
1. Basic Principles in Pharmacology	6.87 (2.95)	10.35 (3.79)	7.73 (3.10)	8.59 (3.67)	3-18	5.03	*
2. Drug Effects on Nervous System	10.86 (3.77)	15.90 (4.91)	10.91 (3.87)	12.87 (5.01)	5-28	8.77	*
3. Psycho-pharmacology	3.87 (1.81)	5.40 (2.21)	3.82 (2.96)	4.52 (2.37)	1-12	2.59	ns
4. CNS Stimulants and Depressants	8.40 (3.16)	9.50 (4.47)	7.18 (3.68)	8.55 (3.92)	2-20	1.28	ns
5. Anesthetics	6.13 (2.69)	4.00 (1.89)	3.00 (1.00)	4.46 (2.35)	1-12	8.33	*
6. Cardiovascular Agents	7.47 (3.76)	11.95 (3.24)	5.82 (2.04)	9.02 (4.11)	3-19	15.73	*
7. Ocular Pharmacology	0.53 (0.64)	0.65 (0.87)	29.82 (12.87)	7.59 (14.00)	0-50	91.66	*
8. Respiratory GE Tract Agents	2.20 (1.97)	3.15 (1.69)	1.91 (1.76)	2.54 (1.85)	0-8	2.08	ns
9. Endocrine Pharmacology	4.20 (2.43)	6.80 (3.58)	5.82 (2.64)	5.72 (3.17)	0-14	3.16	ns
10. Chemotherapy	8.47 (4.14)	13.75 (5.52)	8.27 (4.08)	10.72 (5.40)	0-30	7.10	*
11. Poisons and Antidotes	1.27 (1.22)	3.25 (2.51)	1.27 (1.10)	2.13 (2.09)	0-10	6.24	*
12. Drug Interactions	1.80 (1.01)	1.45 (0.69)	1.73 (0.90)	1.63 (0.85)	0-4	0.81	ns
13. Prescription Writing	1.60 (1.12)	1.05 (0.89)	1.09 (0.70)	1.24 (0.95)	0-4	1.67	ns
14. Total Hours in Pharm	63.80 (19.56)	90.65 (18.36)	94.82 (16.04)	82.89 (22.39)	39-127	12.36	*

*$p < .05$

ocular pharmacology, while dental and medical schools averaged less than one hour. The curricula of schools of dentistry emphasize the pharmacology of drugs that affect sensation and consciousness (defined here as "anesthetics"). As seen in Table 1, a mean of 6.13 hours was devoted to the study of anesthetics in the 15 dental schools responding to the survey. This is statistically ($p < .05$) more hours than the lecture time in medical or optometry schools. This emphasis on anesthetics was also reflected in the earlier study by Kahn and Neidle,[5] which reported means of 5.1 hours in general anesthetics and 4.2 hours in local anesthetics. The total number of hours (9.3) devoted to the subject in 1976, however, was apparently greater than that utilized by the dental schools surveyed herein. Nonetheless, local anesthetics continue to be a mainstay in the practice of dentistry. Many of th complex operative procedures o conscious patients would be im possible without adequate pa control. Also, there is an increasir demand from dental patients fo not only pain-free, but also anx ety-free treatment, and they pref not to remember the procedur Intravenous conscious sedatic and nitrous oxide analgesia co tinue to be an adequate means overcome the fear and anxi y

most patients. Availability of new agents with increased safety and efficacy for use in conscious sedation techniques has enhanced the margin of safety for this means of patient management.[1] However, any practitioner who would employ this pharmacological approach in patient treatment must be thoroughly trained in the pharmacology and clinical application of these drugs.

It is clear from Table 1 that the lecture hours in the dental and optometry schools are remarkably similar, with significant differences occurring only in anesthetics and ocular pharmacology, the latter of which confers a significant difference in the total number of lecture hours between the two professional schools. This similarity is of particular interest since the dentist, who graduates after about 63 hours of instruction in pharmacology, becomes licensed and is allowed to prescribe any drug related to his practice. However, in most states, graduates of optometry schools can use diagnostic drugs only; in several states, they are not allowed to use any drug in their practice.

The medical schools devote significantly more hours to drugs that affect the nervous and cardiovascular systems. Additionally, the medical schools spend significantly more hours than either of the other professional schools in teaching chemotherapy. The scope of treatment in medicine is much broader and requires chemotherapy for microbial, fungal, viral, and parasitic diseases, as well as neoplasia. While the study of antimicrobial and antifungal agents also represent a major proportion of a dental pharmacology curriculum, the scope of treatment in dentistry is more restricted with emphasis on acute orodental infections or antibiotic prophylaxis in patients at risk of developing

Table 2. Comparisons Between School Types for Significant ($p < .05$) Differences on Major Pharmacology Study Categories

		t-ratio	df	t-Probability
Basic Principles in Pharmacology	Dental-Medical	3.06	32.9	.004*
	Dental-Optometry	0.71	21.0	.483
	Medical-Optometry	2.08	24.5	.048*
Drug Effects on Nervous System	Dental-Medical	3.84	33.0	.001*
	Dental-Optometry	0.42	21.5	.675
	Medical-Optometry	3.13	25.3	.004*
Anesthetics	Dental-Medical	2.62	23.9	.015*
	Dental-Optometry	4.13	18.8	.001*
	Medical-Optometry	1.92	29.0	.064
Cardiovascular Agents	Dental-Medical	3.70	27.6	.001*
	Dental-Optometry	1.43	22.4	.165
	Medical-Optometry	6.46	28.3	.001*
Ocular Agents	Dental-Medical	0.46	33.0	.652
	Dental-Optometry	7.54	10.0	.001*
	Medical-Optometry	7.51	10.1	.001*
Chemotherapy	Dental-Medical	3.23	33.0	.003*
	Dental-Optometry	0.12	21.9	.906
	Medical-Optometry	3.14	26.3	.004*
Poisons and Antidotes	Dental-Medical	3.08	29.0	.005*
	Dental-Optometry	0.01	22.9	.991
	Medical-Optometry	3.03	28.1	.005*
Total Lecture Hours in Pharmacology	Dental-Medical	4.13	29.2	.001*
	Dental-Optometry	4.44	23.6	.001*
	Medical-Optometry	0.66	23.3	.518

*$p < .05$

bacterial endocarditis or other complications because of compromised host defense mechanisms. Although there are a number of newer antimicrobial, antifungal and antiviral agents marketed now, the apparent time devoted to these agents currently is less ($\overline{X}$= 8.47 hours) than in 1976 ($\overline{X}$=11.1 hours).[5]

A revealing statistic in this survey was the comparison of the total number of lecture hours in each of the three professional schools. The total hours of pharmacology instruction in the dental schools ($\overline{X}$=63.80 hours) were significantly less than either the medical schools ($\overline{X}$=90.65) or the optometry schools ($\overline{X}$=94.82).

Currently, the time devoted to any subject must be evaluated in terms of the real problem of the ever expanding dental curriculum. The dental curriculum is influenced by outside forces and recognition of new community needs. The dental schools are expected to accommodate new areas (e.g., geriatrics, physical evaluation, ethics, external rotations, medically compromised patients, newly developed drugs) with teaching time, and yet provide adequate clinical experience and a grasp of the basic sciences upon which dental education depends. Other new programs have been proposed in dental epidemiology and statistics.[9] Morris[10] has suggested that perhaps the most serious problem with the dental curriculum, which affects the quality of the education, is that of overcrowding. Hence, suggestions are made "to reduce the mass of information that is taught formally and that the student is required to know"[9] and to reevaluate the basic science content in dental education.[2]

An important question is: are the hours devoted to pharmacology and therapeutics providing adequate training so that the dental graduate today can provide patients optimally with effective and safe drug therapy? It is morally obligatory that excellent instruction and training, at all levels of dental education, be available. This, coupled with the growing concern of overcrowding in dental curricula, makes it imperative that we, as faculty, diligently strive to insure "quality hours" of instruction. We must select judiciously from the expanding biomedical sciences to enrich and strengthen the student's educational program, professional progress and ability to communicate effectively and intelligently with his colleagues in the health care field.

Conclusions

1. Based upon this research, dental schools spend significantly less lecture time in pharmacology than either medical or optometry schools.
2. Optometry schools spend significantly more hours teaching pharmacology for the degree of drug utilization or prescription by that profession.
3. Dental schools devote significantly more lecture hours on drugs which affect consciousness and sensation than medical and optometry schools.
4. Medical schools place great importance on teaching principles of pharmacology, cardiovascular drugs, chemotherapeutic agents and drugs that affect the nervous system.
5. There are no significant differences in time devoted to teaching respiratory and GI tract agents, psychopharmacology, CNS depressants and stimulants, endocrine pharmacology, prescription writing, and drug interactions in the three types of professional schools.

References

1. Montgomery, E.H. and Jeske, A.H., Newer Aspects of the Pharmacology and Physiology of Intravenous Sedation, Journal of Dental Education, 63: 831-956, June 1984.
2. Neidle, E.A., Gies Redux: A Time to Look at Basic Science in the Dental Curriculum, Journal of Dental Education, 49:14-17, January 1985.
3. Dean, D.H., How Do Dental Students Feel About Rx Drugs?, Dental Student, 57:22-23, February 1979.
4. Aviado, D.M., Teaching of Pharmacology. In Pharmacologic Principles of Medical Practice, Baltimore: Williams and Wilkens, 1972, pp. 1207-1214.
5. Kahn, N. and Neidle, E.A., The Teaching of Pharmacology in Dental Schools in the United States and Canada, Journal of Dental Education, 40:541-545, August 1976.
6. AADS Curricular Guidelines in Pharmacology, Journal of Dental Education, 46:176-183, March 1982.
7. Goth, A., Medical Pharmacology, ed. 10, St. Louis, Mosby, 1981, pp. ix-xi.
8. Griedman, G.D., Primer of Epidemiology, New York: McGraw-Hill, 1974, p. 52.
9. Melcher, A.H., Do Faculties of Dentistry Belong in Universities?, Journal of Dental Education, 48:492-495, September 1984.
10. Morris, A.L., Quality of Education, Journal of Dental Education, 47:643-649, October 1983.

Reprint requests to:
Alex Waigandt, Ph.D.
Department of HPER
University of Houston
4800 Calhoun
Houston, Texas 77004

The outcome of interest is the dependent variable

X	X^2
8	64
9	81
7	49
8	64
9	81
5	25
6	36
4	16
7	49
8	64
71	529

$N = 10 \quad \sqrt{\dfrac{529 - \frac{504.1}{10}}{10-1}} \quad \sqrt{\dfrac{529 - 504.1}{9}} = 1.66$

$X_{ll} + (i)\dfrac{N/2 - cumf_u}{fi}$

$\dfrac{10}{2} = $

count ½ way up

X	f	cumf
9	2	10
8	3	8
7	2	5
6	1	3
5	1	2
4	1	1

$(7.5) \dfrac{\frac{10}{2} - cumf_u}{} \quad 7.5 + (1 \times \frac{10}{2} - 5)$

$\dfrac{(7.5 +) + 5 - 5}{} \quad \dfrac{7.5 + 0}{1}$

8.5

Percentile Rank = $\dfrac{cum_u + \left(\dfrac{X - X_{ll}}{i}\right)(fi) \times 100}{N}$

score = $X_{ll} + \dfrac{i(cumf - cumf_u)}{fi}$ = $16 + \dfrac{1(3.5 - 2)}{5}$

$cumf = \dfrac{PR \cdot N}{100}$

$= \dfrac{23.33 \times 15}{100}$

$= 3.5$

$= 16 + .3$
$= 16.3$

Final Examination Homework

no credit - but can bring it

1. In the mini-design, do people from Missouri, Arkansas, or Kansas have higher life satisfaction. "Life satisfaction" is:
   1) the independent variable, nominal in nature
   2) the independent variable, interval in nature
   3) the dependent variable, nominal in nature
   4) the dependent variable, interval in nature ✓

2. For the following distribution of scores: 8,9,7,8,9,5,6,4,7,8, calculate the following:
   the mean = __7.10__ $\frac{\Sigma X}{N}$
   standard deviation = __1.66__ $\sqrt{\frac{\Sigma X^2 - (\Sigma X)^2/N}{N-1}}$
   the median = __7.5__

   $median = X_{ll}(fi)\frac{N/2 - cumf_{ll}}{fi}$

Use the following data to respond to questions 3 and 4:

X	f	cf
22	1	15
~~21~~	~~2~~	~~14~~
20	3	12
18	2	9
17	2	7
16	3	5
15	1	2
14	1	1

$PR = cumf_{ll} + \left(\frac{X - X_{ll}}{i}\right)(fi) \times 100 \over N$

$PR = \frac{12 + (21 - 20.5)(2)}{1} \times 100 \over 15$

$PR = \frac{13.5 + .5}{8} \times 100$ $\quad PR = 86.66$

page 19

3. The percentile rank for a score of 21 is approximately
   a. 75.56
   b. 78.87
   c. 82.33
   d. 86.66 ✓
   e. 95.50

4. For a percentile rank of 23.33, the equivalent score is approximately
   a. 15
   b. 16 ✓
   c. 17
   d. 18
   e. 20

The outcome of interest is the dependent variable.

5. I would like to develop norms with information on three samples. The following data have been collected.

p. 21   365

MxN / N

1st sample	2nd sample	3rd sample
2400 +	3538 +	3003
n = 100	n = 122	n = 143
M = 24	M = 29	M = 21
s = 3	s = 5	s = 6

$M_w = \dfrac{\Sigma(w \times M)}{\Sigma w}$

What is the weighted mean score for the three years? __24.49__

p. 30
x2 see chart

6. What percentage of the area under the normal curve is between z-scores -.50 and .50? __38.3 %__

7. Calculate a Pearson r for the following data.   p. 32   r =

Subject	X	X²	Y	Y²	XY
1	12	144	5.90	34.81	70.8
2	10	100	6.28	39.44	62.80
3	9	81	6.12	37.45	55.08
4	7	49	6.77	45.83	47.39
5	5	25	6.90	47.61	34.50
	43	399	31.97	205.14	270.57

r = __-.95__

8. Calculate the Spearman r for the following ratings. (one is the highest and eight is the lowest)   p. 33

Subject	Rating by Judge 1	Rating by Judge 2	D	D²
1	1	2	-1	1
2	2	1	1	1
3	3	6	-3	9
4	4	5	-1	1
5	5	4	1	1
				13

r_s = __.50__

mistake here

9a.

$$y' = \bar{y} + r \frac{S_y}{S_x}(x - \bar{x})$$

$$y' = 32 + .80 \frac{7}{5}(28 - 25)$$

$$y' = 32 + 1.12(3)$$

$$y' = 32 + 3.36$$

$$y' = 35.36$$

9b. $S_{est\,y} = S_y \sqrt{\dfrac{n(1-r^2)}{n-2}}$

$= 7\sqrt{\dfrac{30(1-.64)}{30-2}}$

$= 7\sqrt{\dfrac{30(.36)}{28}}$

$= 7\sqrt{\dfrac{10.8}{28}}$

$= 7\sqrt{.3857}$

$= 7(.62)$

$S_{est\,y} = 4.34$

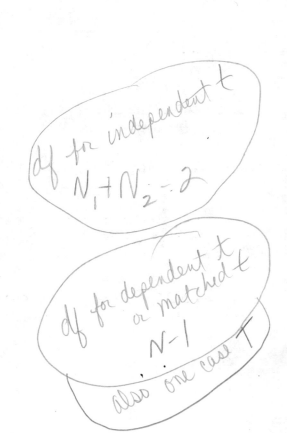

df for independent t
$N_1 + N_2 - 2$

df for dependent t or matched t
$N - 1$
also one case t

in notes

9. The relationship between two variables were scrutinized. The following results were obtained:

X	Y
M = 25	M = 32
sd = 5	sd = 7
X = 28	Y' =

r = .80
N = 30

a. Student x obtained a score of 28 on the X-variable. What is our prediction of his or her score on the Y-variable? __35.36__

b. Determine the standard error of Y. __4.35__

10. An investigator wishes to determine the effects of different degrees of motivation on the performance of a particular task. He employs seven sets of identical twins and randomly assigns them to the two groups. What does he conclude? (Hint: This is a two-tailed test.) *dependent t matched pair* p 41

Group 1 (N=7)	Group 2	D	D²
7	9	-2	4
11	10	1	1
4	8	-4	16
11	9	2	4
9	11	-2	4
7	18	-11	121
12	15	-3	9
		-19	159

$\bar{D} = 2.71$

a. H_o: *There is no significant difference in degrees of motivation in performance*
b. H_1: *There is a significant in degrees of motivation.*
c. Statistical test (be specific): *dependent t*
d. Significance level: __.05__
e. Critical region (~~one~~-tailed test, *two*): $t_{.05} \geq$ __df=6   2.447__
f. Calculated t = (do your calculations below) __-1.70__

N-1
7-1

g. Decision: __We do not reject the H_o.__

$$\frac{(20-27.5)^2}{27.5} + \frac{(30-22.5)^2}{22.5} + \frac{(25-24.75)^2}{24.75} + \frac{(25-20.25)^2}{20.25} + \frac{(30-27.5)^2}{27.5}$$

↑ ↑ ↑
2.045 + 2.5 + .003 + ... $\frac{(20-22.5)^2}{22.5} + \frac{(35-27.5)^2}{27.5} + \frac{(15-22.5)^2}{22.5}$

.227 + ... + 2.045 + 2.5?

= 16.5?

$$\chi^2 = \sum_{r} \sum_{c} \frac{(fo-fe)^2}{fe}$$

where $fe = \frac{\text{row total}}{\text{grand total}} \times \text{column total}$

$\frac{50}{200} \times 110 = 27.5$ $\frac{50}{200} \times 110 = 27.5$

$\frac{50}{200} \times 90 = 22.5$ $\frac{50}{200} \times 90 = 22.5$

$\frac{50}{200} \times 110 = 27.5$ $\frac{50}{200} \times 110 = 27.5$

$\frac{50}{200} \times 90 = 22.5$ $\frac{50}{200} \times 90 = 22.5$

Steve
p. 90

one-tailed = one direction
2 tailed = either way

11. A math instructor was interested in determining whether men students made better marks than women students in math. She randomly selected the final test scores of ten men and women. Is the difference between groups significant at the 5% level?

$\boxed{N_1 + N_2 - 2}$ $N = 10$

Men		Women		X_1	X_1^2	X_2	X_2^2
32	48	38	62	32	1024	38	1444
35	52	43	57	35	1225	43	1849
37	46	38	49	37	1369	38	1444
44	51	39	61	44	1936	39	1521
47	59	46	58	47	2209	46	2116
				48	2304	62	3844
				52	2704	57	3249
				46	2116	49	2401
				51	2601	61	3721
				59	3481	58	3364
				451	20,969	491	24,953

1. a. H₀: *There is no sign. diff. in the math scores of men & women.*
2. b. H₁: *There is a sign. diff. " " " " " " " " "*
3. c. Statistical test (be specific) *independent t*
4. d. Significance level: .05
5. e. Critical region (one-tailed test): $t_{.05} \geq$ *df=18 / 1.734*
6. f. Calculated t = (do your calculations below) *-.99*
7.
8.
9.

g. Decision: _____

12. An investigator was interested in determining the relationship, for student between years at school and feelings about a particular issue. She collected data from 200 students and obtained the following results. Employ the .01 significance level and determine what she concluded.

	In favor	Against	
Freshmen	20 / 27.5	30 / 22.5	50
Sophmores	25 / 27.5	25 / 22.5	50
Juniors	30 / 27.5	20 / 22.5	50
Seniors	35 / 27.5	15 / 22.5	50
	110	90	200

H0: *There is no significant difference in the relationship between* *yrs. in school & feelings about a topic*

H1: *There is a significant difference*

Statistical Test: χ^2 for test of the independence of categorical variables.

Significance level: p. = .01

Sampling distribution: df = __3__   (r-1)(c-1)

Critical region: __11.341__

Do your calculations below: $\chi^2 =$ 10.101

Decision: _____

13. An exercise physiologist attempts to determine if there is a difference in weight loss using three different treatment conditions. Use the summary table below to decide whether or not there are significant differences among the three treatments at the .05 level.

Summary Table

Variance	SS	df	MS	F-ratio
Between Groups	19.22	2	___	___
Within Groups	109.22	40	___	
Total				

Decision: _____.

1. 4   +1
2. 4   +1
3. 3 (45)   +2
4. 4 (11.28)   +2
5. 3   +1
6. 4   +1
7. 1   +1
8. 2   +1
9. .4798 or 45.9%   +1
10. 1 (10)   (-1)
11. .643   +2
12. 2.83   +2
13. 1 reject   +1
14. b decrease   +1
15. d   +1
16. b   (-1)
17. There is no sig. diff. in blood pressure of men & women. +1
18. c independent test +1
19. b Type II   +1
20.
21. nothing   (-1)
22. t = -2.25   do not reject   +2
23. t = (.632)   do not reject   (-1)
24. t = (-1.36) do not reject   (-1)
25. x^2 = 9.98 reject the Ho.

+2

$\frac{54}{59}$

if calculated value is $\geq$ the chart value then there is a significant difference & we reject the H_0.

if the calculated value is $\leq$ the chart value then there is no sig. diff & we do not reject the H_0.